*Freedom, Equality,
and the Market*

Freedom, Equality, and the Market
Arguments on Social Policy

BARRY HINDESS

Tavistock Publications
London & New York

First published in 1987
by Tavistock Publications Ltd
11 New Fetter Lane, London EC4P 4EE

Published in the USA by
Tavistock Publications
in association with Methuen, Inc.
29 West 35th Street, New York NY 10001

© 1987 Barry Hindess

Printed by Richard Clay
(The Chaucer Press), Bungay, Suffolk

British Library Cataloguing in Publication Data
Hindess, Barry
Freedom, equality and the market:
arguments on social policy.
1. Social policy
I. Title
361.6'1   HN17.5

ISBN 0–422–79470–8
ISBN 0–422–79480–5 Pbk

Library of Congress Cataloging-in-Publication Data
Hindess, Barry.
Freedom, equality, and the market.
(Social science paperbacks; no. 349)
Bibliography: p.
Includes indexes.
1. Social policy.   2. Economic policy.
3. Welfare state.   4. Equality.
I. Title.   II. Series:
Social science paperbacks; 349.
HN18.H48   1987   361.6'1   86–14534

ISBN 0–422–79470–8
ISBN 0–422–79480–5 (pbk.)

Contents

Acknowledgements

Many people have helped in the preparation of this book, often inadvertently. Some of its arguments were developed in the course of discussions with students and colleagues at Liverpool University, especially Jane Marceau and Olive Stevenson, and with members of the seminar on State and Politics at Birkbeck College. I am particularly grateful to Paul Hirst, Ann Jungmann, Elizabeth Kingdom, and Sheila Smith, who read and commented on the manuscript.

I

Introduction

In 1981 the OECD published *The Welfare State in Crisis*, a collection of conference papers dealing, we are told, 'with a major contemporary problem. It is important to understand the fundamental nature of the crisis if wrong conclusions and presumptions are to be avoided' (OECD 1981: 5). The same title was used again in 1984, this time for an Open University set book. It begins with the claim that 'the welfare state throughout the industrialised West is in disarray. The outward signs of trouble are of course all too familiar' (Mishra 1984: xiii). Today it is almost a commonplace to say that there is a crisis of the welfare state (but see Klein and O'Higgins, 1985, for a note of caution). Accounts of the nature of the supposed crisis vary considerably. Perhaps the most straightforward is in terms of a combination of demographic and economic changes. On the one hand, the increasing proportion of old people imposes a growing burden of support costs on the working population. On the other hand, the slowdown in economic growth and the rise in unemployment since the 1960s had a considerable impact on expenditure on the social services. The expansion of welfare programmes came to a halt at the same time as increasing demands were made on the welfare services. Improved welfare could no longer be financed out of the increment of economic growth, and the level of welfare expenditure became a matter of political dispute. The question was raised in some quarters whether we could really afford a welfare state on anything like its present scale, and there were fears of tax-payers' revolts.

In other accounts these economic and demographic factors are merely the occasion for a crisis that has more fundamental roots; that is, the problem lies in the very structure of the welfare state itself. On one side the welfare state is seen as a coercive apparatus tending to undermine the workings of a free society. In this scenario individuals are coerced into paying, through taxation, for services that are frequently unresponsive to their particular needs and which they have not personally chosen to use. Furthermore, the welfare state restricts the scope for market-based alternatives to its services so that opportunities for the exercise of freedom of choice are severely limited. From this point of view the crisis of the welfare state is a welcome development. Arthur Seldon, Advisory Director of the Institute of Economic Affairs, argues that the welfare state is an enemy of liberty. At one time it was regarded in Britain 'as not only morally sacrosanct but politically impregnable' (Seldon 1981: 47). By the time he published his pamphlet *Wither the Welfare State*, the situation had changed: 'the welfare state is withering away because it is being undermined by market forces in changing conditions of supply and demand for education, medicine, housing, pensions and lesser components of welfare (Seldon 1981: 11). If the welfare state is to continue, it will have to resort to increasing levels of coercion of consumers and suppliers of welfare services. The British will not tolerate that development, so the state institutions of welfare will eventually wither away.

On the other side is the view that there is an inescapable tension between the welfare and egalitarian principles of the welfare state and the market principles of a capitalist economy. Several versions of this view are discussed in later chapters. For the moment, notice that many on the left see the welfare state, for all its faults, as a little island of socialism in the wider capitalist society, an achievement of the organized working class (and other groups) against capitalist opposition. From this point of view the economic problems of the 1970s and 1980s have strengthened the hand of the other side, thereby providing the occasion for an ideologically motivated attack on the post-war welfare state. The blurb for a book based on a Fabian Society seminar suggests that the welfare state is now 'facing its greatest crisis. Under political attack from the free marketeers, and financial threat from the policies of monetarism and supply-side economics, does the Welfare State have a future?' (Glennerster 1983). The attack, of course, is denied – and that by a government that is cutting back on the real value of many social security benefits and actively encouraging the growth of private medicine and education and the sale of local authority housing. It is not the welfare state, it claims, that is under attack, but only its excessive development.

This is a book of social theory, not another book about the crisis of the welfare state. An important part of what is in dispute between these various accounts of the welfare state and of its supposed crisis is the matter of how we should think about modern British society and the place of government and other social forces within it. This involves questions of social theory – how to analyse society and the relations between its different parts – and questions of political principles or values. These questions are the subject-matter of this book. It discusses the role of public intervention in social and economic processes in modern Britain, with particular reference to the welfare state. The aim is to examine different theoretical and political perspectives on social policy by considering how they depend first on particular conceptions of modern British society and of the place of government and other social forces within it, and secondly, on particular social values or principles and conceptions of the relations between principles and the activities of governments and other agencies.

Discussion of these issues is inevitably contentious. It raises matters of dispute in social theory as well as matters of political disagreement. My own position on many of the issues raised will become clear in the course of discussion, but my primary aim is to exhibit competing views about what kind of theory of society and what political principles are involved, and to analyse what is at stake in the disputes between them. This is a book about arguments, about different ways of analysing British society and the place of social policy within it. Some of the arguments considered here are employed in political debate, but this is not a book about the political struggles around social policy. It makes use of information about British society and the welfare state, but it is not primarily about the institutions of the welfare state or its history. Finally, it is written as an introduction to the arguments rather than a comprehensive survey of the debates. Most of the chapters examine a small number of representative texts in order to show how their arguments work or fail to work, and the problems that arise within them.

Many commentators suggest that, until recently, there was a broad consensus on social policy in Britain. The editor of the Fabian collection referred to above writes of 'the basic assumptions on which social policy has been based' (Glennerster 1983: 1) for most of the post-war period, and which now have to be rethought. On the right, we have noted Seldon's comment that the welfare state was once thought to be impregnable. The first two chapters after this introduction examine that 'consensus' view. Subsequent chapters consider, first, some of the objections that have been raised against it and, secondly, two alternative perspectives that have become significantly more influential in social-policy discussion as the old consensus has broken down.

We begin then with a perspective on social policy that was widely shared by senior politicians, civil servants, and social-policy academics throughout much of the post-war period. In this perspective contemporary British society was seen as the product of two fundamental and interrelated changes. One concerns the character of the economy: the power of the capitalist class has declined, and that of government has expanded. The result is that government can achieve any objective it wishes in relation to the level of employment, income distribution, and the balance between investment and consumption in the economy as a whole. Crosland gives the clearest expression of this view in his book *The Future of Socialism*, published in 1956. He argues that Britain is no longer a capitalist society in the traditional sense, and that with economic power firmly in the hands of government, the eradication of poverty and other socialist objectives can be achieved without significant changes in the pattern of property ownership. Similar views, with rather different ideological undertones, were dominant in the Conservative Party for much of the post-war period. Chapter II thus considers Crosland's argument and some of the difficulties with it.

The other supposed change concerns what Marshall calls the growth of citizenship, a qualitatively new relationship between the state and the underlying population. Marshall argues that the growth of citizenship has produced a broad equality of legal, political, and social rights throughout the adult population. The development of social rights in particular means that all citizens now have a claim to a minimum level of welfare as of right, not as charity. In this sense, citizenship, with its implications for equity, is supposed to conflict with the market principles of capitalist society. Closely related arguments can be found in Townsend's attempt to establish an objective definition of poverty based on concepts of 'participation' and 'relative deprivation' (Townsend 1979), and in Titmuss's account of the conflict of values between social policy and the market. These views are considered in Chapter III.

If we take these two supposed changes together, it must seem that the only real obstacles to the eradication of poverty and a more egalitarian society are the government's lack of knowledge of social conditions, on the one hand, and its lack of political will, on the other. These assumptions underlie much of the 'Fabian' critique of social-policy provision, and a whole tradition of social administration research (see Donnison 1979; or 1982, Ch. 2, for a good short account). The discussion here and in the rest of the book will consider questions of how far modern Britain can indeed be characterized in terms of these changes, whether there is more to the failure of egalitarian welfare policies than ignorance and lack of political will, and whether what the welfare state does is best analysed primarily in terms of equity and the distribution of welfare.

Following the economic policy failures of successive British governments in the 1960s and 1970s, problems for the consensus view became increasingly apparent. Crosland's optimistic picture of the capacity of government to manage the economy is now widely disputed on both the left and the right of British politics. Some of these arguments are considered towards the end of the book. But first we consider two other kinds of objections that have been made against the consensus view. The first is that the changes which once made the consensus view appear plausible have potentially destructive consequences in the longer term. Chapter IV considers Goldthorpe's argument that the combination of citizenship and economic growth in a capitalist economy leads to the emergence of a mature working class willing and able to use its power to secure inflationary increases in real wages, thereby undermining the political and economic conditions of the consensus. We shall see that Goldthorpe's account of the British inflation of the 1970s displays a striking sociological reductionism. For all his insistence on the social antagonisms underlying Britain's inflation, he pays little attention to the political conditions in which those conflicts are conducted.

Chapter V considers a more general argument to the effect that the consensus view generates a style of politics that is ultimately self-destructive as the 'logic of the situation' leads sectional interests to make demands on government, and it leads political parties to compete for their support with promises of action. There are several versions of that argument. In this book we concentrate on Beer's discussion in *Britain Against Itself* (1982) and on the liberal argument that 'unlimited democracy' generates a 'new Hobbesian dilemma', a competitive struggle between sectional interests for state intervention in their favour. We shall see that the argument from the 'logic of the situation' in an interventionist state suffers from many of the weaknesses of Goldthorpe's sociological account of Britain's inflation.

The second set of objections to the consensus view are based on the observation that public expenditure on social-service provision has markedly inegalitarian consequences. Our interest here is not so much with the evidence, which is generally unambiguous. It shows that in many areas of public-service provision the overall effect of public expenditure is to exacerbate the significance of differences in income and wealth. Rather, we are concerned with the political conclusions that have been drawn from this evidence, especially with regard to what le Grand (1982), following Tawney (1931), calls 'the strategy of equality'. That strategy involves moving towards social and economic equality by means of public expenditure on social services, on education, health, housing, and transport. The conclusion drawn by le Grand is that 'the strategy of equality' has clearly failed, and therefore that a far more radical attack on privilege is required. This argument raises important questions regarding the uses of social principles, such as equality, in the assessment of policies and social conditions. We shall see that the political implications of the evidence are by no means as clear-cut as le Grand and others suggest.

Finally, Chapters VII and VIII consider two alternative approaches to the analysis of social policy that have become considerably more influential with the collapse of the old consensus. Marxism analyses politics and the state primarily in terms of the struggle between contending classes. The welfare state therefore appears both as serving the interests of the capitalist ruling class and as an island of socialism in the sea of capitalist society, brought about and defended by working-class struggle. Considerable ingenuity is devoted to attempts, never entirely successful, at resolving the tension between these two positions.

In many respects the approach of liberalism to the analysis of social policy could not be more different. Liberal political thought is concerned to establish limits to the role and power of the state, seeing the growth of the state as posing a threat to individual freedom and privacy, with potentially damaging consequences for economic activity and for social life generally. Recent liberal writing on the welfare state has insisted on the need to minimize state economic intervention and on the disruptive effects of removing responsibility for welfare provision from the individual and family. In effect, an apparent concern for the liberty of the individual is given priority over all other social and political objectives. Where Marxism operates with a relatively systematic theory of social structure and social change, liberalism's interest in social structure is primarily because of its supposed consequences for the liberty of the individual. Liberals do have something to say about social structure, but it is generally crude and simplistic. The problem here is obvious enough in the vulgar polemics of Friedman and the Institute of Economic Affairs, but it can also be found in the otherwise more serious and sophisticated work of Hayek.

There are, of course, alternatives to the consensus view other than those based on Marxism and liberalism. The most far-reaching of these, in terms of their theoretical and political ramifications, relate to feminism. Feminism gets little mention in most general discussions of approaches to social policy, and this book is no exception, but there is a growing feminist literature on a whole range of issues relating to social policy. These issues certainly need to be discussed, and the fact that they are not considered here does not mean that they are unimportant. Any book on social theory will take up some issues and not take up others that have a bearing on its argument. In this case, there are two reasons why a chapter on feminism would not have been appropriate. First, I am concerned with two inter-related themes that recur throughout the positions considered in this book and which give it a certain unity. These themes concern first an essentialism of the market, shared by Marxists, liberals, and most of the other positions considered here, and secondly the question of the place of principles in political discussion and the analysis of social conditions. Feminism raises important issues for any politics concerned with the principle of equality, but it does not do so primarily in relation to the essentialism of the market that characterizes the other positions considered here.

The second reason is more significant. The unequal treatment accorded to men and women, important though it is, is not the only issue raised by feminist discussion of social policy. Feminism has also brought to the fore fundamental questions of the place of gender in relation to other features of social life, and, in modern society in particular, of the role of the state and other social-policy agencies in fostering certain patterns of gender relations and of domestic organization. In the course of her argument that the welfare state can be defined as 'the State organisation of domestic life' (Wilson 1977: 9), Wilson quotes from the Beveridge Report of 1942 as follows: 'the attitude of the housewife to gainful employment outside the home is not and should not be the same as that of the single woman. She has other duties' (1977: 151). There can be little doubt that what I have called the consensus view does involve powerful, and often unexamined, conceptions of gender relations and of desirable forms of domestic organization. The same is true of the other positions considered here – although the situation has begun to change in recent years as liberals have tried to counter feminist arguments, and Marxists to accommodate (at least some of) them. To have considered here – although the situation has begun to change in covered in this book would have required not just another chapter (feminism as a third alternative to the consensus view) but also a radically different treatment of the consensus view in Chapters II and III, and of the positions discussed in subsequent chapters. It would have made for a different, more complex kind of book, and perhaps for a better one. It would certainly have been much longer.

The two recurrent themes are taken up in the concluding chapter. The first concerns the essentialism of the market. For all of the striking differences between them, Marxism and liberalism both tend to analyse the market in terms of an essence or inner principle that produces necessary effects simply by virtue of its presence. Of course, they arrive at this essentialization of the market and its workings in rather different ways. In the one case it is a sign of exploitation and the anarchy of capitalist production; in the other case it is an index of freedom. But in both, market and plan appear as distinct and incompatible principles of social organization, so that any combination must appear to be inherently unstable. Different but closely related oppositions between the market and the principles of social welfare and citizenship can be found in the works of Marshall and Titmuss, discussed in Chapter III (e.g. Marshall 1950, 1981; Titmuss 1958, 1970), and again in Goldthorpe's account of Britain's inflation (Goldthorpe 1978). Wherever it appears, the essentialism of the market involves a serious weakness in the shape of a failure to take account of the institutional conditions within which particular markets operate. The result is that simplistic generalizations about the market and its supposed antitheses are altogether too prominent in many accounts of social policy.

The second recurrent theme concerns the place of principles in political discussion and the analysis of social conditions. In social-policy discussion principles may be invoked both as an explanation of social conditions and as a means of evaluating them. This is clear enough in the case of Hayekian liberalism, where social conditions and policies are analysed in terms of their supposed consequences for the liberty of the individual. Or again, the principle of equality is used by le Grand both as an explanation of British social policy and as a measure of its success. Finally, the arguments of Marshall and Titmuss involve the analysis of social conditions in terms of a conflict between the principles of citizenship or altruism and the unprincipled workings of the market. There are, of course, differences in the ways in which principles are used in these examples, but they all raise similar general issues of the place of principles in the assessment of social conditions and in the evaluation of proposals for change.

In fact the analysis of social conditions in terms of the realization of principles depends on an essentialism not unlike the one we have noted with regard to the market. To analyse social conditions or policies solely in terms of the realization of some general principle is to ignore the unavoidable complexity both of social conditions and of attempts to change them. Principles do indeed play a part in political life, but they do so always in conjunction with a variety of other concerns, interests and objectives. Political parties and governments act in terms of existing institutional conditions and social forces which invariably restrict their room for manoeuvre in certain respects. Some of those conditions may well be changeable as a result of political action, but many have to be regarded as more or less fixed, at least in the short term. It makes no sense to analyse societies or parts of them in terms of the realization of general principles.

That point has serious implications for the use of principles in the evaluation of the success of policies and political strategies. If society cannot be organized as the realization of a single general principle, then governments and political parties cannot reasonably be blamed for failing to bring about that state of affairs. Consider le Grand's argument that 'the strategy of equality' has failed and that therefore a more radical attack on the sources of inequality is required. The argument takes the fact of discrepancies between British social conditions and the principle of equality as a measure of egalitarian failure. The evidence here is pretty well decisive. What is not so clear are the political conclusions to be drawn from it. Inequalities are to be expected, and they will come about for a variety of different reasons. They will not be equally matters of political concern or equally amenable to political action.

Serious assessment of policies involving egalitarian or other principles depends on an analysis of the political and institutional conditions in which those policies have been pursued and of the obstacles that they confront. It does not follow from the continued existence of inequalities in our society that 'the strategy of equality' should be scrapped, or that the gestural alternatives are likely to be more successful. The argument, then, is not that principles have no place in the evaluation of social conditions and policies. Quite the contrary. The point rather is that social conditions and policies intended to change them cannot be evaluated in terms of principles alone. The evaluation of proposals for reform should be a complex matter in which considerations of equality, freedom, or whatever, appear as one element together with a variety of other considerations. The alternative is a naive political radicalism, with limited purchase on current political conditions or possibilities.

This last point has been made in terms of equality, but it could equally well be made in terms of other principles, for example, liberty, fraternity, or solidarity. But a word of warning is in order before concluding this introduction. To say that there are simplistic political analyses conducted in the name of equality, and others in the name of liberty, is not to say that these naive radicalisms are equivalent. Naive political radicalism comes in many shapes and sizes, and its effects are not all of a kind. What those effects are depends on the objectives it sets itself, their relation to other concerns and objectives, the political forces that act on its proposals, and, of course, the obstacles that stand in its way. Simplistic political analyses are all too common on the left, and that is part of the reason for its weakness. The tradition of broadly egalitarian social-policy writing, from which le Grand draws much of his material, is responsible for some of those analyses. But it has also produced some excellent research studies and well-informed, severely practicable proposals for change in particular areas of social policy. At its best, it has contributed to the development of a more effective 'strategy of equality'. The more naive egalitarianism has had little direct impact on the practical conduct of national or local government. Unfortunately, the same cannot be said of that pursuit of individual liberty which appears to override all other objectives. That naive radicalism is altogether more dangerous.

II

Government and the economy

Here and in the following chapter we examine a perspective on social policy that was widely shared until recently by senior civil servants and politicians of all parties. In this perspective contemporary British society appeared as the outcome of two fundamental changes. One concerns the growth of citizenship, which we consider in Chapter III. The other concerns the character of the economy and the power of government within it. The claim is that government can now achieve any reasonable objective concerning the level of employment, the distribution of income, and the level and pattern of investment. This chapter considers one of the clearest expressions of this claim and some of the problems with it.

THE TRANSFORMATION OF CAPITALISM AND THE FUTURE OF SOCIALISM

The writings of Anthony Crosland occupy an important place in post-war British politics. Crosland is remembered as a leading figure among the Labour Party 'revisionists' of the 1950s and 1960s, and as an important, if often frustrated, member of Labour cabinets until his death in 1978. His major work is *The Future of Socialism* (1956), but its main themes were introduced in his contribution to *New Fabian Essays* (1952) and subsequently qualified and elaborated in *The Conservative Enemy* (1962) and *Socialism Now* (1974). Crosland's books and articles provide a clear account of the proper aims of a modern social democratic, or Labour, party and of how they might be achieved. As the central text of Gaitskellite revisionism, *The Future of Socialism* made a major contribution to factional debate within and around the Labour Party. But it also has a more general significance for the understanding of post-war British politics.

First, it lays out a very clear conception of the capacities of governments with regard to economic management in Britain and other advanced Western societies. Crosland argues that these capacities are relatively new, and that they have been brought about by significant transformations of capitalism. He also provides one of the best discussions of the political implications of these capacities, especially with regard to the problems of bringing about social reforms without provoking widespread resistance. This is obviously an important issue for anyone on the left in a parliamentary democracy.

Now, although Crosland wrote as a socialist, the conception of the capacities of government for economic management that he outlined was widely shared by Labour and Conservative leaderships until at least the late 1960s. It is still influential in the Labour Party, the SDP, and the Tory left and centre. We shall see later that this view of the capacities of government and of their political implications provokes deep hostility on both the right and the left. It is disputed on the right because it is said to lead to inefficiency and the supplanting of entrepreneurial initiative in the economy, to the making of excessive demands on the political process and to problems of government overload. It is disputed on the left on the grounds that it fails to understand the fundamental character of capitalism. Both sides share the conclusion that Crosland grossly overstates the effective capacity of government economic management. The political and economic history of Britain over the last twenty years or so has also generated a profound popular scepticism about the prospects of government economic management (Alt 1979) quite independently of the arguments of Crosland's liberal or Marxist critics.

Secondly, *The Future of Socialism* raises and discusses many issues that have come to the fore in subsequent political debates. Since public services have to be financed by charges for their use or from government revenues (and ultimately therefore taxation), Crosland recognizes that there may be a political problem of maintaining support for high levels of government spending on public-service provision. Writing in a period of economic growth, Crosland was optimistic about this. Or again, he recognizes that government commitment to the maintenance of full employment may involve the risk of inflation. Here, too, given his views on government economic management, Crosland is relatively optimistic. Finally, in relation to the public sector, we find Crosland floating ideas now generally associated with the Labour left. For example, he advocates a public investment bank, to direct investment where private capital is clearly failing, and the formation of competitive public enterprise as an alternative to nationalization. There are 'left' versions of these proposals in Stuart Holland's *The Socialist Challenge* (1975) and in *Labour's Programme, 1973* and subsequent editions.

Thirdly, many passages in *The Future of Socialism* clearly express an irritation with the Labour left that has played an important part in Labour politics since the war. It is an irritation with what Crosland regards as the posturing and sloganizing character of much left politics. In effect, it is a reaction to a style of politics that has characterized parts of the Labour left since at least the late 1940s. Consider, for example, this comment on the Bevanite disputes of the early 1950s:

> 'It is difficult to argue that they were *about* anything real, or that the so-called Right and Left were genuinely divided by serious, clear-cut policy differences. . . . This bitterness is only a reflection of a curiously strong tendency within the Labour Party towards a suspicious, militant class-conscious leftism. . . . Mr. Bevan only articulated a resentment which was already there.'
>
> (Crosland 1956: 94–5)

We will return to this 'resentment' below. The irritation which Crosland so clearly expresses was one of the elements in the Labour Party battles leading up to the split of 1980 and the formation of the SDP.

But for present purposes the crucial feature of Crosland's discussion is his argument concerning government capacities to manage the economy and their political implications. The structure of the book gives a good indication of how Crosland's argument works. Part One is called 'The Transformation of Capitalism' and the remainder deals with the implications of that supposed transformation. Part Two, 'The Aims of Socialism', argues that the transformation of capitalism requires a serious rethinking of the socialist project. This section contains one of the clearest modern statements of the argument that socialism is about equality. There follow sections on 'The Promotion of Welfare' and 'Equality', discussing class, social justice, education, the distribution of income and wealth, and the organization of industry, and on 'Economic Growth', as a precondition for the pursuit of welfare and a more egalitarian society.

The Future of Socialism raises many issues that cannot be considered here. What matters for our purposes and for the foundations of Crosland's argument is the supposed transformation of capitalism discussed in Part One. He begins by suggesting that pre-war socialists had assumed, first, that major reforms would be impossible short of the overthrow of capitalism, and secondly, that the collapse of capitalism was imminent. Both, he argues, are false: capitalism shows no sign of collapsing, and there has been a significant shift of economic power away from the capitalist class.

'First, certain decisive sources and levers of economic power have been transferred from private business to other hands; and new levers have emerged, again concentrated in other hands than theirs. Secondly, the outcome of clashes of group or class economic interests is markedly less favourable to private employers than it used to be. Thirdly, the social attitudes and behaviour of the business class have undergone a significant change, which appears to reflect a pronounced loss of strength and self-confidence.'

(*ibid.*: 26)

On the first point the main changes concern the growth of the public sector, including the post-war nationalizations, and government acceptance of the responsibility for economic management:

'Acting mainly through the Budget, though with the aid of other instruments, the government can exert any influence it likes on income distribution, and can also determine within broad limits the division of total output between consumption, investment, exports and social expenditure.'

(*ibid.*: 27)

Government can also exert 'a powerful influence on production decisions in individual industries' (*ibid.*: 27) through the use of various incentives and controls. Finally, although Crosland does not develop the point, there had been a marked change in the technical capacity of British governments to intervene. This involved not just the wartime controls (most of which were subsequently dismantled) but also the development of statistical machinery for monitoring exports, imports and the cost of living, an expanded tax base and a massive expansion of government borrowing.

Crosland's other two points concern the balance of political forces in relation to the economy. The effect of full employment, and of the commitment of Labour and Conservative parties to maintaining it, is a permanent shift of power from management to labour. 'Even under Conservative Government the Trades Unions remain effective masters of the industrial scene' (*ibid.*: 94). Or again: 'One cannot imagine today a deliberate offensive alliance between Government and employers against the Unions . . . or, say, a serious attempt to enforce a coal policy to which the miners bitterly objected' (*ibid.*: 32–3). Further, the growth of large corporations, both public and private, has reduced 'the power of the capitalist class relative to other managerial classes' (*ibid.*: 33) and, of course, relative to government.

In effect, then, Crosland's view is that modern governments can regulate the overall level of economic activity through fiscal policy, their own spending power, and their role as by far the largest borrower in the financial markets. It was the widespread belief that governments could do that, and that they could therefore be held responsible if they did not, that made unemployment such a sensitive political issue for most of the post-war period. In addition, Crosland maintained that governments could use taxation and other policy instruments to control the balance between consumption and investment, thereby determining the rate of growth, and to regulate the post-tax distribution of income.

The net effect of these changes in the powers of government and the associated shifts in the balance of political forces amounts to a 'national shift to the left [which] may be accepted as permanent' (*ibid.*: 28–9). Government should no longer be seen as the executive committee of the capitalist class: 'economic power will, in fact, belong to the owners of political power. And these today are certainly not the pristine class of capitalists' (*ibid.*: 29). Indeed, 'by 1951 Britain had, in all essentials, ceased to be a capitalist country' (*ibid.*: 42). For this reason, Crosland argues that ownership is no longer particularly significant in determining the character of our society. The socialist attack on poverty, inequality, and the chronic instability of capitalism does not require any massive transformation of the pattern of economic ownership.

Crosland draws two conclusions from this point about ownership. First, as a general policy, nationalization is irrelevant to the pursuit of socialist objectives. He is not opposed to nationalization in principle, and indeed he strongly supports nationalization of basic utilities and of certain basic industries. Thereafter, he maintains that any proposal for further nationalization must be justified. The main consideration here concerns the capacity of government to control the industry in question. Would public ownership add significantly to the powers government already has in the form of fiscal policy, investment grants, and so on? Here Crosland raises a severely practical objection against the claim that nationalization is necessary as a crucial means of placing power in the hands of government. This claim was one of the major planks in the Labour case for further public ownership, and it is still influential on the left of the party.

Crosland's response is very clear. First, the record of government management of the nationalized industries is not impressive. In the post-war period planning 'proved scarcely easier to achieve under public than private ownership' (ibid.: 466). Secondly, government does not require ownership as a means of exercising control. 'The truth is that there is now no insuperable economic difficulty about the Government imposing its will, provided it has one, on either private or public industry' (ibid.: 468). We shall see that there are good reasons to doubt this second point. But the fact remains that the advocates of extended public ownership in Britain have yet to show that public ownership would represent an effective and significant addition to the powers that governments already have to cajole, direct and otherwise influence the behaviour of private industry.

The second conclusion Crosland draws from the irrelevance of ownership concerns the importance of profit. Socialists have traditionally been hostile to private profits. But if we maintain a substantial private sector, then profits are necessary as a source of new investment and as a condition of economic growth. The problem for socialists is not to reduce or eliminate private profit, but rather to ensure that it is used mainly as a source of collective capital formation and not as a form of personal income. Crosland's argument is that governments can use fiscal policy to regulate the uses to which profit is put. Private profit is to be made into an instrument of government economic management.

POLITICAL IMPLICATIONS

In effect, Crosland's argument is that there has been a radical transformation in the position of government in relation to the British economy. Government is now in a position to so regulate the distribution of resources as to ensure a reasonable level of economic growth under conditions of full employment, to move towards a more equitable post-tax distribution of income, and to expand the level of public spending on social-service provision. There is therefore no general case for further expansion of public ownership as a means of enhancing government control of economic activity. It follows that socialist objectives have to be reconsidered. In particular, the abolition of private ownership of productive property is no longer a significant part of the socialist programme. Other elements should come to the fore in its place. The major objectives, in Crosland's view, are the elimination of poverty, inequality, and the chronic instability of capitalist economic life. The third has already been achieved, and the first is well under way: 'We stand, in Britain, on the threshold of mass abundance' (*ibid*.: 515).

The primary domestic objective of British socialism must therefore be the pursuit of equality. But why should equality matter in the society of mass abundance that Crosland (in 1956) sees as Britain's future? In *The Future of Socialism* he gives several reasons, of which two are particularly important. One is that persistent inequalities generate strong collective resentments that can have serious political and economic consequences. We have seen how Crosland interprets the Bevanite disputes of the 1950s partly in these terms. But he also suggests that much of Britain's industrial unrest must be understood as a consequence of resentments induced by social inequality. Crosland is obviously not alone in this objection to inequality. The idea that inequality is a problem for British society because it generates resentment and therefore conflict is an important theme in the books written by Shirley Williams and David Owen on leaving the Labour Party.

However, that simplistic sociological account of resentment is only part of the reason why Crosland is a committed egalitarian. Equality is important as a basic moral value, a principle of social justice that Crosland regards as common to all the major traditions of socialist thought. The pursuit of equality is ultimately a matter of principle. The political problem facing socialists in Britain is therefore how to move towards a more egalitarian society under conditions of parliamentary democracy. The redistribution of wealth, income, and power, has to be brought about in such a way that it does not generate a level of electoral resistance that would result in the return of a Conservative government. The democratic pursuit of equality can operate at several levels. First, the maintenance of full employment and the existence of strong trades unions can minimize power differentials between management and workers. Secondly, there should be a concerted attack on inherited wealth and other large holdings of private property. This would strike at only a tiny minority of the population. It would not affect earned incomes or small holdings of property. Resistance to such an attack is unavoidable, but it need not be an electoral liability for a reforming Labour government.

But what of the remaining inequalities, relating to earned incomes and access to education, health, and other socially desirable resources? The suggestion here is that in a period of economic growth, the increment of growth can be used both to expand public services and to effect a redistribution of incomes after tax without provoking much resistance on the part of the better-off. To the extent that social services and redistribution are financed out of government tax revenues, it is necessary to avoid politically unpopular tax increases. In *Socialism Now*, after years of relatively slow growth, Crosland reinforces this point. Socialist objectives:

'require a redistribution of wealth and resources; and we shall not get this unless our total resources are growing rapidly. I do not of course mean that rapid growth will automatically produce a transfer of resources of the kind we want; whether it does or not will depend on the social and political values of the country concerned. But I do dogmatically assert that in a democracy low or zero growth wholly excludes the possibility. For any substantial transfer then involves not merely a relative but an *absolute* decline in the real incomes of the better-off half of the population (which incidentally includes large numbers of working class voters); and this they will frustrate . . . ultimately by using the ballot box to elect a different and more lenient government.'

(Crosland 1974: 74)

Increases in the level of income tax or of domestic rates can provoke political opposition, and opposition to the services they are supposed to pay for. Crosland's argument, therefore, is that the effective government pursuit of egalitarian policies presupposes economic growth. In its absence, we should expect pressure to cut back on services that are currently provided for the old, the sick, and the unemployed.

Whatever we think of Crosland's specific argument on this point, he does raise a serious issue that many on the left ignore. Egalitarian politics pursued through the expansion of public services and income redistribution runs the risk of alienating electoral support. Successful socialist politics, in Crosland's terms, requires the implementation of egalitarian programmes without losing elections:

'Since there are limits to the amount of additional revenue which the Government can raise, both the attainment of a rapid rate of growth and the avoidance of inflation (not to mention the winning of elections) require that the Party should show some restraint in its election promises, and should have a clear view of its priorities in the field of government expenditure.'

(Crosland 1956: 409)

Socialists who denounce such restraints take a cavalier and irresponsible attitude to the political conditions of parliamentary democracy: 'In a utopia (or a dictatorship) perhaps we might transfer x per cent of a near-static GNP towards eight million pensioners, better housing and clearing up pollution; in the rough democratic world in which we live, we cannot' (Crosland 1974: 74).

We will return to the question of the use of public spending as a means of securing social justice and equality at several points throughout this book. First, it relates to the second change that the consensus view supposes to have taken place in Britain; namely, the growth of citizenship and of state responsibility for welfare. Secondly, of course, it is taken up by numerous critics of Crosland and the consensus view. Some of the more substantial of these will be considered in later chapters, but there are some responses, popular on the left, that are particularly worth noting at this point.

CROSLAND AND HIS CRITICS

There is obviously something fundamentally wrong with Crosland's arguments. We have noted his optimism about economic growth, the capacity of government to manage the economy, the changed balance of power between management and labour, the 'permanent' shift of British politics to the left, and so on. Some of these assertions were disputed at the time (e.g. in reviews of *The Future of Socialism* by Hutton and Strachey), but in the light of Britain's experience over the last twenty years or more they must now seem remarkably anachronistic. Crosland himself later recognized that *The Future of Socialism* was too complacent regarding economic growth. In *Socialism Now* he notes two problems with his earlier views. First, demographic changes imposed greater demands for housing, education, and other resources than he had anticipated. Secondly, 'I did not anticipate that successive governments would be so eccentric as to use periodic bouts of deflation, that is, deliberate *reductions* in growth, as almost their only means of regulating the economy' (1974: 73). There is something to be said for the first point, but the second is more problematic. No doubt incompetence (or eccentricity) has played an important part in government economic policy throughout the post-war period. But, as Arblaster notes, for Crosland to use that as the major explanation for the failure of his complacent projections is clearly unsatisfactory (Arblaster 1977: 421).

It is not difficult to use events since 1956 to show that Crosland was mistaken. To show where he went wrong, what it is in his arguments that is unsatisfactory, is more difficult. It is a task that is often evaded by left-wing critics of the revisionism of Crosland and his associates. For example, in *Socialism with a Human Face* (1982) Meacher dismisses Crosland with the observation that there is little in his principles that is not compatible with the continued existence of capitalism. It follows that whatever may be said for Crosland's principles, they don't amount to socialism. The precise definition of socialism is clearly open to debate. But since Crosland makes his case on the basis of the supposed transformation of capitalism, Meacher's dismissal amounts to little more than an evasion of Crosland's central arguments.

Arblaster's assessment is more serious, since he does try to show that Crosland's 'transformation' of capitalism is an illusion. Writing in the year of Crosland's death, he claims that the 'analysis on which revisionism was founded has been fatally undermined by the actual history of British capitalism in the past quarter of a century' (Arblaster 1977: 417). Perhaps – but that is a dangerous argument for a Marxist to employ. Even so, the differences between Crosland's projections and the actual course of events do not suffice to pinpoint the weaknesses in the analysis on which those projections were based. (The same point can be made against those critics who would dismiss Marx's arguments on the grounds that his predictions have not materialized.) Unfortunately, rather than address Crosland's arguments in any detail, Arblaster treats the manifest failures of his projections as justifying the wholesale rejection of the gradualist strategy of British revisionism: 'It was the logical product of a fundamentally wrong, and over-sanguine, account of the supposed transformation of British capitalism into a system more stable, more humane and enlightened, more rational and controlled' (*ibid.*: 427).

There are two points to notice about that assessment of Crosland's revisionism. First, what the socialist alternative to gradualism might be under conditions of British parliamentary democracy remains unclear – and it is not difficult to see why. Secondly, Arblaster's conclusion, that British capitalism has not been transformed, may or may not prove correct, but it does not follow from the obvious bankruptcy of Crosland's complacent projections.

There are indeed problems with Crosland's arguments concerning the transformation of British capitalism, and we will come to some of them shortly. For the moment, notice that there is another left response to Croslandite revisionism which tries to advance its case on the grounds that things have changed. For example, in *The Socialist Challenge* Holland argues that the 'Keynesian' techniques of economic management advocated by Crosland and his associates are no longer sufficient because of the rise of meso-economic power. Or again, the left-wing authors of *Manifesto* tell us that

> 'after the war western governments had reached a high point in their power to control the economic system. They were able to plan spending, investment and employment and to control trade, exchange rates and finance. Today almost the opposite is the case.'

(Cripps et al. 1981: 24)

Crosland may have been all right in his time, but the world has changed! The implication is that institutional changes are necessary so that British governments would once more have the powers that Crosland and others claimed for them. To this end, *Manifesto* aims to make Britain 'an independent, self-governing country within the free world' (*ibid.*: 9) by, for example, leaving the EEC and negotiating a 'new pattern of international relationships' (*ibid.*: 15).

Leaving aside the specific proposals of these authors, there is a real problem with a form of argument that rejects a particular political and/or economic analysis on the grounds that the world has changed. Of course the world has changed in important respects. It would be most disturbing if it had not. Such truisms may have their place, but they are no substitute for serious argument. All too often this claim, that the world has changed, functions as a convenient device for refusing to address the strengths and weaknesses of particular arguments about the character of British, or any other, society. This is certainly the case with Crosland's treatment of the arguments of 'pre-war' British socialists, and of some of the opposition to his views in the post-war Labour Party. In the way that he fails to address the arguments of those whose analyses he rejects, Crosland leaves open the possibility that they may once have been correct – and, of course, he invites the response that capitalism has not *really* changed. Much of the sterile debate around the British revisionism of the 1950s and 1960s turns on the failure of either side to seriously address the arguments of the other. In fact, the central arguments of *The Future of Socialism* are generally rather weak, and the fact that it had such an impact is a good index of the quality of discussion in British political life.

As for the rejection of Crosland's position on similar grounds, that too may suggest that his analysis was all right in its time. This, like much of the Marxist response to Crosland, represents a serious failure to come to terms with the strengths and weaknesses of his specific arguments. One result is that Crosland's complacent assessment of the capacities of British governments to manage the economy is transposed onto the state of affairs that would exist if only certain institutional changes were introduced – a bit more nationalization, planning agreements backed by the threat of public ownership, leaving the EEC, and so on. Such changes may be desirable on other grounds, or they may not. What they cannot do is restore a state of affairs that has never obtained. Post-war British governments have indeed had at their disposal a considerable array of means of intervention in the operations of the British economy, but these have not had quite the characteristics that Crosland claimed to find in them.

'GOVERNMENT CAN EXERT ANY INFLUENCE IT LIKES'?

In fact, there are very good reasons for doubting that the high levels of economic growth and of employment enjoyed by the advanced Western economies in the early post-war period were the result of 'Keynesian' interventions on the part of their governments (Matthews 1968). If Matthews's argument is correct, then the state of Britain's economy in the 1950s cannot be cited as proof of government capacity to maintain full employment and economic growth. But, whatever the outcome of that debate, there are serious problems with Crosland's account of post-war British governments' capacities for economic management: 'the government can exert any influence it likes on income distribution, and can also determine within broad limits the division of total output between consumption, investment, exports, and social expenditure' (Crosland 1956: 27). And again, there 'is now no insuperable economic difficulty about the Government imposing its will, provided it has one, on either private or public industry' (*ibid.*: 468). There are no doubts here about the ability of government to manage the economy as it sees fit. If there are problems, they are problems of political will, not administrative capacity or economic power.

Crosland's view of the capacities of government has been disputed, in rather different ways, by the Marxist left and by the liberal right. Some of their arguments will be considered in later sections of this book. We shall see that they suffer from an essentialism (of capitalism as a mode of production, or of the market as a principle of social organization) that vitiates much of their analysis. Nevertheless, without falling into these essentialisms, it is possible to show that the capacity of government to act in pursuit of its economic (or other) objectives is always subject to definite limitations.

First, there are important features of British economic life not within the control of the British government. For example, the British economy is unusually dependent on foreign trade. We import about half of the food we consume and a high proportion of the raw materials used in manufacturing. Britain is also a large exporter and importer of manufactured goods. The balance of trade imposes a real constraint on the freedom of action of British governments since it depends in part on the willingness of foreign companies and governments to buy what Britain wishes to sell. Of course, governments can and do intervene to affect the pattern of trade, sometimes successfully, but the outcomes of their interventions are not entirely within their control. Similar points may be made with regard to international capital movements, dealings in sterling and other currencies, interest rates abroad, and so on.

But the more general problem with Crosland's view concerns the relationships between policy instruments and objectives. Governments pursue objectives, economic or otherwise, by means of a particular set of policy instruments. For example, the system of personal taxation is used to collect revenue to finance government activities. It may also be used to affect the post-tax distribution of income, or to encourage certain patterns of savings and expenditures and to discourage others. Thus tax relief on mortgage interest payments encourages home ownership and, until recently, tax relief on life insurance premiums encouraged savings linked to life insurance. Government may attempt to influence private industry through taxation, through a variety of grants and specific tax reliefs, through the indirect effects of hire purchase controls, and so on. Each of these instruments will have a definite organizational structure and means of action. That is, it will depend on the activities of specific governmental and non-governmental organizations. For example, the system of personal taxation depends both on the work of the Inland Revenue and on the co-operation of private and public employers in the PAYE system.

At any given time, then, a government will have at its disposal a particular set of policy instruments, each involving specific organizations and means of action. This point has serious implications for Crosland's account of the power of government to manage the economy. First, because each instrument depends on specific organizations and means of action it will have its own particular strengths, weaknesses, and limitations. For example, there are clear limitations on the capacity of governments to increase their revenues through the imposition of high rates of personal taxation. The problem is not simply that they may lead to electoral resistance. They also encourage a variety of legal and illegal devices for avoiding payment. Policy instruments are not automatic relays for translating government intentions into reality. Their effectiveness depends on the organization of the instruments in question and the responses to their actions on the part of a variety of actors (individuals, private and public corporations, other government agencies). Since these actors are subject to infuences and conditions that are not themselves wholly determined by government and its policy instruments, their responses cannot be entirely guaranteed.

Secondly, at any given moment the set of policy instruments available to government is effectively given. New instruments may be created and existing ones modified, but substantial changes in the current set of instruments take time to implement, and they are by no means always easy to achieve. Meanwhile governments must make do with the existing set of instruments to pursue their immediate and short-term policy objectives. There is then an obvious temptation to use particular instruments in pursuit of a variety of distinct and not entirely compatible objectives. The British tax system is a good example of this problem (see Kay and King 1978). Again, the use of a policy instrument in pursuit of one objective can have repercussions for other government objectives. For example, the use of interest rates as a means of shoring up the value of sterling in international currency markets directly affects the cost to government of financing its own borrowing requirements. It may also have consequences for the money supply, the level and pattern of industrial investment, mortgage interest rates, and so on.

These points illustrate the general argument that the capacity of governments to pursue their policy objectives will always be subject to the limitations of the policy instruments available to them. Although it has been developed here in relation to economic policy, the argument clearly applies to government policy in other areas. We shall see that it has important implications for the consideration of social policy.

The existence of limitations is not something that may be overcome, in the area of economic policy, by the expansion of public ownership. Even in the public sector governments can pursue their objectives only through the use of specific policy instruments. Some of those instruments will differ from those deployed in relation to the private sector, but they will nevertheless have their own limitations. In that respect there are always difficulties about the government 'imposing its will' on private or public industry. Of course, the repertoire of policy instruments is not fixed, and it may be changed through political action. But new instruments and significant changes to old ones can rarely be introduced overnight or without cost. Crosland is absolutely right to insist that, compared with pre-war Britain, post-war governments had a vastly increased capacity for action in pursuit of (at least some of) their policy objectives. But it does not follow that they were not subject to any limitations at all, as many of his remarks suggest.

This argument is important for several reasons. First, Crosland's extravagant claims allow his opponents to claim an easy victory by pointing to the many manifest failures of British government policy in the post-war period. Arblaster (1977) suggests that the state does not yet have the power it needs to control the economy. Here the failures of government economic management are presented as effects of the capitalist character of the economy. Arblaster goes on to argue that the issue of public ownership must therefore return to the socialist agenda. In fact, British economic policy failures show nothing of the kind. What they do show is that the policy instruments available to British governments, and the way they were deployed, did not measure up to their policy objectives. It might perhaps be claimed that that problem is itself the result of the essentially capitalist character of the economy, but merely pointing to those policy failures cannot establish that conclusion.

Secondly, failure to relate policy objectives to the instruments and organizational means by which they might be pursued has been a chronic weakness of British political debate. Cairncross's study of British economic policy from 1945 to 1951 suggests that few Labour ministers understood the requirements of economic planning. The government's handling of the 1947 fuel crisis was a particularly striking example of incompetence in industrial planning by a government committed to economic planning in principle (Cairncross 1985).

Again, for all the rhetoric of planning in the late 1950s and 1960s there is considerable evidence to suggest that both Conservative and Labour leaderships used their economic plans more as public relations devices, aimed at securing wage restraint and greater investment, than as serious instruments for pursuing their proclaimed objectives (Lereuz 1976). Labour's 1965 'plan', developed in the Department of Economic Affairs, and the earlier Conservative NEDC 'plan' both seemed to confuse forecasting exercises with serious attempts at planning. It would be misleading to suggest that Crosland was entirely unaware of the problem here. In his later career he was clearly concerned that Labour should consider its objectives in relation to the organizational and other means of achieving them. Nevertheless, since the bulk of the argument of *The Future of Socialism* rests on his claims regarding the ability of government to manage the economy as it·sees fit, his failure in that book to consider the problems of economic management in relation to the available policy instruments and their limitations, must be considered a serious weakness.

THE BALANCE OF POLITICAL FORCES

Finally, we should note some problems with Crosland's assessment of the balance of political forces in contemporary Britain. Three issues are particularly significant here. First, part of Crosland's argument concerning the loss of power by the capitalist class and the irrelevance of ownership, rests on the growth of large private and public corporations. These represent a loss of the 'power of the capitalist class relative to the managerial class' (Crosland 1956: 33) and, in the case of the public sector, a direct transfer of capitalist power to the state. Here Crosland takes up the 'managerialist' thesis that the growth of large corporations involves a transfer of power into the hands of a new class, whose interests differ from those of the old-style capitalists. That thesis has been the subject of considerable debate which cannot be considered here (but see Scott 1979; Tomlinson 1982). But, whatever one thinks of Crosland's managerialist position, the declining significance of individual human capitalists tells us nothing about the power of large corporations. The power of the individual human capitalist may have declined, relative to other centres of power in the economy, but it does not follow that the power of large holdings of private property has similarly declined. In *The Future of Socialism* Crosland has remarkably little to say about the powers of large corporations (as distinct from the power of managers within them), and even as late as *Socialism Now* he denied that large corporations pose any special problems for British governments.

Crosland's position on this point has been disputed by Holland who, in *The Socialist Challenge*, stresses the importance of meso-economic power in the modern world, and by the authors of *Manifesto*, who emphasize the political power of private capital. There are certainly problems with some of their arguments, but they do suggest that Crosland may have been too hasty in concluding that ownership was irrelevant. Political parties and voters are not the only influences on the policies of governments. Trades unions and employers' associations, large enterprises and financial institutions, and a variety of other agencies, may also have a significant impact. Crosland's assertions regarding the capacity of government to use taxation and budgetary policy to regulate the behaviour of private industry clearly raises the question of the capacity of some of those threatened with regulation to organize political opposition. In this respect at least, his argument for the irrelevance of ownership is more than a little naive.

The other two issues concern Crosland's claim that economic growth is a precondition for any serious democratic politics of redistribution. While the better-off half of the population may be persuaded to accept a relative decline, they would resist any absolute decline in their real incomes. The two points we should question here are, first, the familiar 'levelling-up' argument, and secondly, Crosland's view of what is required to avoid politically-damaging resistance by the better-off. The levelling-up argument is simply that if greater equality is achieved by maintaining the living conditions and standards of the privileged while improving those of the underprivileged, then the privileged have no cause for complaint. There is obviously something to that argument. In the case of household amenities such as piped water, power for cooking and heating, bathroom and toilet, there is no reason why the rich should object if the rest of us have them too. The problem is that not all privileges regarding access to goods and services are of that kind. Hirsch refers to goods that are 'positional' in the sense that their utility to their possessors depends on their not being available to others: 'unspoilt' holiday resorts, first-class rail travel, educational privilege (Hirsch 1976). To take the last example, if certain kinds of education provide relative advantages, then it is impossible to have an egalitarian educational system without removing some of those advantages. There is a further difficulty here. In so far as the development of a more egalitarian education system involves changes in educational institutions (e.g. comprehensivization of secondary education), it may provoke fears over the lowering of educational standards. Such fears may or may not be justified, but they may nevertheless be politically significant. Attempts to equalize the distribution of positional goods threatens to make them less valuable to their possessors. They may provoke resistance on the part of the privileged and the invention of new devices to preserve their privileged positions. 'Levelling-up' financed out of the increment of growth may well prove effective in some cases, but it cannot always be relied on to avoid resistance on the part of the privileged.

Finally, what of Crosland's claim that low growth 'wholly excludes the possibility' of a significant redistribution of resources to the less well-off sections of the community? The argument is particularly important in the light of present British conditions, since it suggests that questions of redistribution should be set aside until we have got the economy right. It is possible to question Crosland's position here in at least two respects. First, it is not clear that the better-off half of the population, including the better-off sections of the working class, will always resist any reduction in their real incomes. François

Mitterrand was elected to the French presidency on a programme that called for sacrifices on the part of the employed population in order to help finance a programme of industrial reconstruction and a reduction in unemployment. In Sweden, the LO (the major trades union federation, organizing mainly blue-collar workers) has practised a policy of wages solidarity for many years. This involves keeping wage differentials to a moderate size and some sacrifices in their wage increases by workers in the more profitable companies. These examples show that it may be possible to win support for policies that clearly involve sacrifices. The more general point to make here is that maintaining or improving real incomes is only one of the concerns that may affect support for a policy or party. People may be concerned, for example, about the long-term effects of mass unemployment on their own quality of life, or about the job prospects for their children. They may well be prepared to put up with some sacrifice of real incomes if it is clearly linked to progress on other issues of real concern.

Secondly, the attainment of even a moderate level of sustainable economic growth in Britain can no longer be seen as a technical problem of economic management, something to be considered independently of significant changes elsewhere in British society. Resources cannot be transferred into investment without some constraint on consumption. It is far from clear that a transfer on the scale required can be achieved without some redistribution of incomes. Any programme of economic reconstruction to improve international competitiveness and to reduce unemployment must secure the compliance of groups whose resistance could seriously undermine that programme – senior management in the large public and private corporations, shop stewards, union officials and workers in key sectors of private industry and parts of the public sector. Paul Hirst and I have argued elsewhere (Hindess and Hirst 1983; Hirst 1985) that the policies of confrontation as practised by the present government (against the unions) or as favoured by sections of the left (against financial institutions and large corporations) are unlikely to prove successful. Governments may well win their confrontations, but with damaging economic effects and disastrous implications for economic growth.

A transfer of resources into investment for economic reconstruction, to say nothing of repairing and improving social-service provision, must require some restraint on incomes. That is unlikely to prove acceptable if it is justified merely on technical economic grounds, and it could not be imposed for long without severe economic consequences. The British labour movement has always been ambivalent about equality, but egalitarian ideas still have significant popular appeal. We have argued that a programme of economic reconstruction is most likely to receive sustained support if it is clearly linked to egalitarian policies of redistribution and to significant improvements in social-service provision. That argument may be disputed, but it does at least suggest that the changes necessary to achieve sustainable economic growth cannot be considered independently of the wider pattern of social relations in British society. In that respect, it can be misleading to present economic growth as necessarily coming before significant changes elsewhere.

III

Citizenship and the market

The second major change that was supposed to characterize post-war British society concerns relations between the state and the underlying population. At its simplest, this change involved the assumption by government of responsibility for social welfare and the development of the welfare state. But what is most distinctive in the perspective we are examining here is the way these developments are represented in terms of a broad equality of rights within the community. Marshall presents the argument in terms of the growth of citizenship, a process of equalization of civil, political, and social rights throughout the adult population. The social component of citizenship implies a claim to a minimum level of welfare as a matter of rights, not of charity. In this sense, citizenship, with its implications for equity, is supposed to come into conflict with the market principles of capitalist society. Different but closely related positions can be found in Titmuss's discussions of the conflict between the market and the principles of social welfare, and in Townsend's attempts to construct a definition of poverty in terms of exclusion from the social life of the community (Townsend 1979). In this chapter we concentrate first on Marshall's argument, which is in many respects the clearest of these positions, and indicate later how it relates to some of the arguments of Titmuss and Townsend.

CITIZENSHIP AND SOCIAL CLASS

Marshall's basic argument concerning the growth of citizenship is set out in *Citizenship and Social Class* (1950). It was published in 1950, after the major social-policy reforms introduced by the post-war Labour government, but before there was much experience of their workings. His account of British society as combining political democracy, social welfare, and a predominantly market economy is developed in some of his later essays, especially 'Value Problems of Welfare Capitalism', and its 'Afterthought: The Hyphenated Society'. We begin with *Citizenship and Social Class*.

Marshall argues that citizenship has three components. The civil component involves those 'rights necessary for individual freedom' (Marshall 1950: 10), and it was particularly significant for the development of the market relations of a capitalist economy. The political component concerns the right to participate in the exercise of political power. Finally, the social component of citizenship covers 'the whole range from the right to a modicum of economic welfare and security to the right to share to the full in the social heritage and to live the life of a civilised being according to the standards prevailing in the society' (*ibid.*: 11). He suggests that these components were interconnected in the feudal period but then parted company and developed separately and at different periods. Very approximately, we can assign the development of 'civil rights to the eighteenth, political to the nineteenth, and social to the twentieth' centuries (*ibid.*: 14).

The details of Marshall's historical account need not concern us here. But two features of his conception of citizenship are particularly important. First, he presents citizenship as a status involving a broad equality with regard to the rights and duties with which it is endowed. All citizens are equal in their capacities as citizens: 'Social class, on the other hand, is a system of inequality . . . It is therefore reasonable to expect that the impact of citizenship on social class should take the form of a conflict between opposing principles' (*ibid.*: 29). This presents us with the apparent paradox that the growth of citizenship 'coincides with the rise of capitalism, which is a system, not of equality, but of inequality' (*ibid.*: 29). How could these opposed principles develop side by side?

Marshall proposes to resolve this paradox in two ways. First, he distinguishes two types of class system. One, characteristic of Britain in the feudal period, is based on legal and customary statuses, so that there are few commonly held rights and class differences have a normative justification in the customs and values of the society. Citizenship has a destructive impact on this type of class system which clears the way for the development of generalized commodity relations in the economy. The other kind of class system is a characteristic of modern capitalism. It is seen by Marshall as a by-product of 'the institutions of property and education, and the structure of the national economy' (*ibid.*: 31). In this system, class differences are not a function of well-defined statuses, and they have no generally accepted normative justification. The growth of the modern class system presupposes the extension of at least the civil component of citizenship. We shall see that this conception of the shift from a normatively based class system to one that is fundamentally amoral plays an important part in Goldthorpe's argument concerning the inflationary consequences of the growth of citizenship.

Secondly, Marshall argues that the rapid growth of capitalism, which generated the modern class system, took place in the nineteenth century. The development of citizenship up to that time did not conflict with the inequalities of capitalist society because it was mainly a matter of the equality of civil rights. In effect, then, the real conflict of principle between citizenship and the modern class system comes with the development of the political and social components of citizenship. The growth of political rights generates a tension between participation in government in the public sphere and exclusion from it in the economic sphere. The suggestion here is that lack of rights with regard to economic power will be seen as more of a problem once there is a basic equality of political rights. There is also a tension between the equality of social rights and the inequalities generated by the market. Marshall refers to the role of trades unions in using their collective civil rights to bring a system of social and political rights and principles of justice into the sphere of capitalist economic relations.

The growth of citizenship, in Marshall's account, did not inhibit the development of a capitalist market economy in Britain. Nevertheless, there is now a clear conflict of principles between them. In the concluding section of *Citizenship and Social Class* Marshall presents the issue as follows:

'[This] conflict of principles springs from the very roots of our social order in the present phase of development of democratic citizenship. Apparent inconsistencies are in fact a source of stability, achieved through a compromise that is not dictated by logic. This phase will not continue indefinitely. It may be that some of the conflicts within our social system are becoming too sharp for the compromise to achieve its purpose much longer.'

(ibid.: 84)

In effect, then, we have conflicting principles of social organization, with British society exhibiting an uneasy compromise between the two.

The idea that there is a conflict between the social principles of the welfare state and the market principles of the capitalist economy is by no means peculiar to Marshall's work. It can be found in numerous discussions of social policy on both the left and the right. Some of these will be considered in later chapters. It can also be found in a rather different form in the work of Richard Titmuss (e.g. 1958, 1970), which we turn to below. Where Marshall differs from many of these other positions is in his positive evaluation of the post-war British compromise. Where Titmuss and the various left- or right-wing critics of the welfare state argue for the primacy of one set of principles over the other, Marshall wishes to maintain the compromise between them. It may turn out that it cannot be sustained, but Marshall would prefer the compromise to continue.

The most forceful statement of Marshall's position on this point comes in 'The Hyphenated Society', published in 1981 as an afterthought to his 1972 essay, 'Value Problems of Welfare Capitalism'. The 'hyphenated society' is that of democratic-welfare-capitalism, where the hyphens indicate that the political, welfare, and economic sectors are to be considered both as interdependent and as partially autonomous. They are autonomous because each is organized around a distinct axial principle. To the extent that these principles have primacy in separate spheres of social life, they are able to remain complementary and interdependent rather than divisive. Marshall prefers this state of affairs to the dominance of any one principle. He argues that the attempt to change the present hyphenated compromise in favour, say, of social welfare would be counter-productive: 'The hyphenated society can survive only if it is recognised that both the welfare sector and the mixed economy are contributing to the creation of welfare' (Marshall 1950: 131). Subordination of economic activity to the demands of social welfare would have disastrous consequences both for economic freedom and for efficiency. Further-more, 'it is hardly possible to maintain democratic freedom in a society which does not contain a large area of economic freedom' (*ibid.*: 135). In terms of Marshall's argument, of course, the main danger of the 1980s is that the welfare sector will lose its status as an equal partner in the tripartite post-war structure. He concludes by insisting on the need to strengthen 'the civilising power of welfare' and to combat the 'anti-social elements in the capitalist market economy which still persist in the mixed economy' (*ibid.*: 135).

CITIZENSHIP AND SOCIAL INTEGRATION

The second important feature of Marshall's conception of citizenship concerns its role in the integration of society. Citizenship generates 'a direct sense of community membership based on loyalty to a civilisation which is a common possession. It is a loyalty of free men endowed with rights and protected by a common law' (*ibid.*: 40–1). This notion of civilization as a common possession involves much more than a simple equalization of civil and political rights. It also includes the ability to participate more or less equally in the social life of society:

'The extension of the social services is not primarily a means of equalising incomes. In some cases it may, in others it may not. . . . What matters is that there is a general enrichment of the concrete substance of civilised life, a general reduction of risk and insecurity, an equalisation between the more and the less fortunate at all levels. . . . Equality of status is more important than equality of income.'

(*ibid.*: 56)

And again:

'The unified civilisation which makes social inequalities acceptable, and threatens to make them economically functionless, is achieved by a progressive divorce between real and money incomes. This is, of course, explicit in the major social services, such as health and education, which give benefits in kind without any ad hoc payment. . . . The advantages obtained by having a larger money income do not disappear, but they are confined to a limited area of consumption.'

(ibid.: 81)

It will be necessary to return to this supposed divorce between real and money incomes. We shall see in Chapter VI that far from reducing the advantages of larger money incomes, public expenditure on the social services often tends to enhance those advantages.

For the moment, notice how something very like Marshall's 'civilisation as a common possession' appears in Townsend's attempt to construct an objective measure of poverty in terms of a concept of relative deprivation. The first step is to measure the distribution of all types of resources which contribute to the standards of living of individuals or households. These resources will certainly include wealth and income from employment and investments, but they will also include resources provided in other forms – public services, company cars and other perks associated with certain kinds of employment, and so on. But, Townsend argues, inequalities cannot themselves suffice to provide a measure of poverty. What is also required is an assessment of how access to resources affects abilities to participate in the life of society. The crucial step in the objective measurement of poverty is therefore:

> 'to endeavour to define the style of living which is generally shared or approved in each society, and find whether there is . . . a point in the scale of the distribution of resources below which, as resources diminish, families find it particularly difficult to share in the customs, activities and diets comprising their society's style of living.'

(Townsend 1979: 60)

In terms of Marshall's discussion, the poor are those whose resources do not allow them to participate in the civilization which the rest of us enjoy 'as a common possession'. For all their possession of civil and political rights, the poor are deprived of an essential component of citizenship. In this sense, the elimination of poverty in modern Britain would be a matter of extending the social component of citizenship to a deprived minority.

To present the relationship between Townsend's relative deprivation measure of poverty and Marshall's conception of the social component of citizenship in these terms is also to point to a common area of difficulty. Both arguments suppose, first, that a generally shared 'civilization' or 'style of life' can be clearly identified, and secondly, as a consequence, there is a well-defined category of persons who fall outside it. On the first point, Piachaud argues that there are intractable problems in attempting to distinguish the effects of differences in taste from those of differences in income (Piachaud 1981). In reply, Townsend claims that 'there is a much stronger material or economic basis than hitherto supposed for what has come to be dismissed as "diversity of taste"' (Townsend 1981: 478). Perhaps. But Townsend's point merely compounds the difficulty. To the extent that differences in taste (regarding, say, skiing holidays or visits to the opera) do depend on differential access to resources, then the notion of a 'style of life' shared by the vast majority of society becomes increasingly problematic. This brings us directly to the second issue. It may be necessary to identify the poor for the purposes of public policies aiming at the relief of poverty. But it does not follow that there must be a single criterion of poverty, let alone a distinctive subculture or life-style that is shared by all those identified as poor. If there is a diversity of styles of living that is itself dependent on access to resources, then we can hardly expect to find a well-defined threshold separating the poor from the rest of us: 'The poor are worse off than others; but for the most part, they are members of society, not outcasts' (Piachaud 1981: 421).

Piachaud does not at all deny that there is real poverty in Britain. But he does dispute the possibility of an 'objective' definition in terms of the lack of opportunities to participate in society's 'style of living'. In his view, the definition of poverty, in the sense of a range of resource constraints that should not be tolerated, is a matter of value judgement or political decision. As for Marshall's concept of citizenship, if it is difficult to identify a 'style of life' shared by the vast majority, then it must be equally difficult to identify a 'civilization' which is a common possession. In that sense (we shall find others) it is surely misleading to describe the welfare state as underpinning the social component of citizenship.

SOCIAL POLICY AND THE MARKET

In Marshall's argument the distribution of goods and services in post-war Britain is characterized by a compromise between two conflicting principles. First there is citizenship. It operates as a principle of equality with regard to law, politics, and participation in the social life of society. This last is particularly important for Marshall's treatment of social policy. His argument supposes that there is a general pattern or style of life in society, a shared civilization, in which everyone, by virtue of their citizenship, has a right to participate. In particular, they should not be excluded through lack of resources. Social policy has the function of ensuring at least the minimal level of equality presupposed by the social component of citizenship. Its aim is not to eliminate economic inequality but to reduce its significance through publicly provided services. We have seen that something similar is involved in Townsend's proposals for an objective, relative-deprivation, measure of poverty. Social policy is a sphere in which resources are allocated on moral grounds. In conflict with the principle of citizenship is the principle of class, in which resources are allocated through the market, through money and monetary exchanges. The pattern of distribution generated by the market has no generally accepted normative foundation. In Marshall's argument the class system is fundamentally amoral.

Marshall's argument is distinctive not so much in its identification of a conflict of principle but rather, as we have noted, in its positive evaluation of the compromise between them. In this respect, the work of Titmuss marks a striking contrast. The conflict of principles is still there, but in Titmuss's view it is clear that the moral values enshrined in social policy ought to predominate. If the two principles conflict then social policy must interfere with the pattern of distribution effected by the market. But the problem comes with interference in the other direction, with the market continually threatening to undermine both the operation of social policy and the values which sustain it. This is a recurrent theme throughout Titmuss's work. It is most clearly stated in his last major work, *The Gift Relationship* (1970), which takes blood donation as exemplifying fundamental principles of social policy.

At one level the argument of *The Gift Relationship* is that the system of blood donation, as a free gift, provides a generally superior product to that of commercialized blood provision. Titmuss supplies a great deal of evidence and argument in support of that position, and he even finds support from private medicine. For example, much of Chapter 9, 'Blood and the Law of the Marketplace', is devoted to a discussion of the Kansas City Case (1962) in which a commercial blood bank invoked anti-trust legislation against an agreement by local hospitals to take their supplies from a non-commercial, community blood bank. Titmuss cites evidence from representatives of private hospitals supporting that arrangement on the grounds that it was generally safer for donors and recipients alike. He notes the irony of the AMA and private hospitals arguing for the non-commercial blood bank in spite of their own general support for private medicine.

But Titmuss's main concern is with another level of argument entirely. It aims to draw the line between the operations of social policy and the operations of the market, taking the supply of blood as an extreme case:

> 'blood as a living tissue may now constitute in Western societies one of the ultimate tests of where the "social" begins and the "economic" ends. If blood is considered in theory, in law, and is treated in practice as a trading commodity then ultimately human hearts, kidneys, eyes and other organs of the body may also come to be treated as commodities to be bought and sold in the marketplace.'
>
> (Titmuss 1970: 158)

And again, '[if] blood as a living human tissue is increasingly bought and sold as an article of commerce and profit accrues from such transactions then it follows that the laws of commerce must in the end prevail' (*ibid.*: 171).

In effect, the argument is that if blood can be turned into a commodity, then nothing is sacred. In that case, Titmuss maintains, there is no coherent basis for social policy:

> 'Where are the lines to be drawn – can indeed any lines at all be pragmatically drawn – if human blood is legitimated as a consumption good? To search for an identity and a sphere of concern for social policy would thus be to search for the non-existent. All

policy would become in the end economic policy and the only values that would count are those that can be measured in terms of money and pursued in the dialectic of hedonism. Each individual would act egoistically for the good of all by selling his blood.'

(ibid.: 12)

That would have disastrous consequences, not only for the forms of social-policy provision but also for the values that underlie it. Titmuss insists on distinguishing between the 'social' and the 'economic' in the field of welfare because of his concern for the ways in which

'specific instruments of public policy encourage or discourage, foster or destroy, the individual expression of altruism and regard for the needs of others . . . providing and extending opportunities for altruism in opposition to the possessive egoism of the market-place.'

(ibid.: 13)

Here, as with Marshall, the 'economic' is seen as an amoral sphere, while that of 'social' provision becomes, in contrast, a sphere of moral choice and intervention. The altruism of social policy is in constant danger of subversion by the egoism of the market.

This brings us to a second theme that Titmuss shares with Marshall. If citizenship has an integrative role, then anything that undermines it poses the threat of social disintegration. We have noted this theme in Titmuss's treatment of the market as a sphere of egoism, which continually threatens to undermine the altruism and social solidarity of the 'social'. As another example, consider his discussion of the effects of private pension and insurance schemes, and of tax concessions to the better off in 'The Social Division of Welfare' (1958). Not only do they have inequitable consequences in providing preferential treatment for the more prosperous, but also, and more seriously, they threaten to undermine the 'unity of social policy', 'for in effect their whole tendency at present is to divide loyalties, to nourish privilege, and to narrow the social conscience as they have already done in the United States, in France and in Western Germany' (Titmuss 1958: 52). The result in Titmuss's view is that the 'aims of equity, ostensibly set for society as a whole, become sectional aims, invariably rewarding the most favoured in proportion to the distribution of power and occupational success' *(ibid.: 55).*

THE AIMS OF SOCIAL ADMINISTRATION

We return below to Titmuss's important essay, 'The Social Division of Welfare'. For the moment, consider the consequences of bringing together this view of the nature of social policy and the view of government's capacity to manage the economy considered in the previous chapter. Taken together, these provide an account both of what the aims of social policy should be and of the political and economic conditions in which it is pursued. Social policy should have the objective of ensuring that all citizens have the capacities and resources needed to participate in the social life of our society. Governments are, or can be made to be, motivated by citizenship considerations. If they are able to manage the economy so as to ensure a reasonable level of economic growth, then it should be possible to finance social policy without generating resistance on the part of the majority of the electorate. Under these conditions it must seem that the only serious obstacles to the realization of citizenship are, first, ignorance of social conditions and, secondly, lack of political commitment on the part of government.

I have suggested that these assumptions underlay an influential tradition of reformist social-policy analysis which presupposes a certain complicity between social scientists, policy-makers, and social-service professionals and administrators. In his inaugural lecture, 'Social Administration in a Changing Society', Titmuss defines the academic discipline of social administration as 'the study of the social services whose object . . . is the improvement of the conditions of life of the individual in the setting of family and group relations' (Titmuss 1958: 14). On the one hand, the role of the social scientist is to inform the policy-makers, to establish the facts of poverty and inequality, and to identify the failures of social service provision:

> 'we cannot expect to achieve a better relationship between the services provided and the needs of a changing society without more knowledge of both; of the nature of social needs and of how the services actually work as distinct from how they are supposed to work.'
>
> (*ibid.*: 28)

On the other hand, Titmuss suggests that it is necessary to identify the interests opposed to the proper development of social policy and to criticize successive governments for their social-policy failures. Here Marshall's 'citizenship', Townsend's 'poverty', or Titmuss's 'social policy' defines a standard against which a society and the performance of its government can be measured. Titmuss's 'The Social Division of Welfare' is an influential example of this style of analysis, and we return to its argument in a moment.

The credibility of this once-influential model of social policy and the role of social administration has been undermined both by the economic failures of successive British governments and by critical arguments from the left and the right, some of which are considered in later chapters. The record of British economic management since the 1950s suggests that there is something wrong with Crosland's account of the capacity of government to manage the economy – or else that successive British governments have been extraordinarily incompetent in their conduct of economic policy. Some of the problems with Crosland's account have been considered in Chapter II.

There are also severe problems with the analysis of the distribution of goods and services in terms of a conflict of principles, between citizenship and social policy, on the one hand, and the market, on the other. If there is indeed a conflict of principles, then, *pace* Marshall's arguments for peaceful co-existence, we should expect the extension of citizenship to have potentially damaging consequences for the operation of the market sector. We might also expect to find resistance to the extension of citizenship on the part of those who benefit from the market system. We return to that issue in our discussion of attempts to explain the failure of the alleged egalitarian promise of the post-war welfare state.

But there is a more serious problem here in the attempt to analyse contemporary Britain, or any other society, in terms of the co-existence of conflicting principles. In this chapter we have seen that Marshall and Titmuss both consider social policy in terms of a principle of social organization that is in conflict with the market, and the idea that there is a conflict between social policy and the market is clearly one that is widely shared on the left and the right in contemporary debate. That approach raises problems at two levels. First, there are problems with the role of the specific principles invoked in the analysis, with the principle of citizenship or social policy, on the one hand, and that of the market, on the other. Secondly, there are general problems to do with the analysis of social conditions as the more or less adequate realization of principle. We will return to these problems in later chapters. For the moment, we note some further problems with the principle of citizenship or of social policy as a tool of social analysis.

'THE SOCIAL DIVISION OF WELFARE'

We have seen that 'The Social Division of Welfare' invokes a specific conception of the coherence of social welfare as a basis for its critique of the effects of private health and insurance. In effect, anything that undermines the coherence of the welfare system is presented as socially divisive. Here a specific principle of social analysis (social policy or citizenship) provides a standard for the evaluation of social conditions in terms of the extent to which they realize that principle or depart from it. But it is also important to notice that there are elements in 'The Social Division of Welfare' itself which tend to undermine the analysis of social policy in terms of any single principle.

Titmuss begins with the observation that there is not one welfare system in Britain today but rather three: public welfare, provided by the state social services; fiscal welfare, constituted by a network of tax concessions and benefits; and occupational welfare, provided for their employees by many private and public employers. Consideration of all three systems gives a very different impression of the overall impact of the welfare state than does consideration of the public system alone. First, the effect of concentrating on the system of public welfare is to give a misleading impression of the redistributive effects of the welfare state. In particular, the fiscal and occupational systems generally benefit the better-off. Unlike means-tested public provision, Titmuss notes that occupational welfare schemes operate as 'concealed multipliers of occupational success' (Titmuss 1958: 137). Thus, even if the public welfare system were egalitarian in its effects, it would not follow that the overall distributional effect of the welfare state was egalitarian.

Titmuss argues that the image of the welfare state which identifies it with the public system produces a misleading stereotype of it as operating to the benefit of the poor and as paid for by the rest of us. This is misleading, first because it ignores the fiscal and occupational welfare systems, and secondly because, as we shall see later, important parts of the public system favour the better-off rather than the poor. Nevertheless, the misleading stereotype does have important consequences. It provides the foundation for right-wing critiques of the welfare state in terms of its alleged redistributive consequences and its effects on incentives. It also affects the self-image of the poor themselves – and of the rest of us. In effect, what appears to be a system of equity serves as a smokescreen for the pursuit of sectional interests.

These points imply, as Sinfield suggests in his equivocal homage to Titmuss's essay, that it may be a mistake to think of 'a single welfare ethic which is at odds with capitalist society' (Sinfield 1978: 153). To characterize British society in terms of one principle of citizenship or welfare or altruism that inevitably conflicts with the market is to ignore fundamental questions about different forms and levels of provision. The point here is not to say that the limited egalitarianism of citizenship is irrelevant, for it clearly plays an important part in political campaigns and programmes. The point rather is that no one principle of welfare describes the overall effects of the various systems of provision.

Secondly, Titmuss suggests that welfare systems generate 'interests' around the various forms of preferential treatment; for example, around mortgage tax relief and occupational pension schemes. Here the 'interests' are seen as being defined amongst the recipients of welfare, although in other writings Titmuss clearly recognizes that welfare professionals might also constitute significant interest groups. But there is a related position on the right, which uses the supposed generation of interests as an argument against public provision. In effect, the argument is that public-service provision creates interest groups amongst its own employees, who aim to serve themselves rather than the public. We consider that position in Chapter VIII. For the present, notice that while Titmuss raises the question of sectional interests and their impact on social policy, it makes little sense to consider this independently of the more general problem of how welfare systems relate to the political institutions, forces, and struggles of British society. Sinfield claims that Titmuss neglects the role of 'class conflict as crucial in creating the overall balance of political forces' on the enactment of social legislation and its form (Sinfield 1978: 146). Whether or not we accept Sinfield's presentation of the issue in neo-Marxist terms, there remains a real problem about how the treatment of welfare in the arguments of Titmuss or Marshall relates to the institutions and processes of British politics. In particular, there is a clear tension between the analysis of social policy as the expression of a principle, and its analysis as the outcome of political struggles.

Finally, there is the question of how far social policy can be analysed in terms of its distributional consequences alone; for example, in terms of the alleviation of poverty or the allocation of welfare. We have seen, for example, Titmuss's argument that occupational welfare schemes frequently operate as multipliers of the effects of occupational success. He also notes that they involve a significant element of control, since the receipt of benefit and its level depend on good behaviour and on continuity of employment. Titmuss notes this point but does not develop it. Nor does he make the related observation that supervision and control plays an important part in much of the public-welfare system. The point here is that social-policy provision is rarely just a matter of the allocation of goods and services as an alternative or a supplement to market provision.

Returning to an argument of the previous chapter, social-policy provision can operate only through definite policy instruments, which have consequences over and above their purely allocative function. In terms of Marshall's notion of citizenship, for example, it is tempting to analyse the system of compulsory education as attempting to provide future citizens with the capacities to participate in the social life of our society. But it clearly does much more, and other, than that. Not only is it far from egalitarian in the education it offers but it also involves a considerable exercise of control and regulation. Or again, Foster notes that the welfare sector does not depend primarily on price as a distributive device:

'Welfare providers . . . have therefore had to devise various forms of administrative rationing to control surplus demand for limited goods and services. . . . Not only does this process play a key role in determining an individual's access to welfare services and benefits, it may also play a significant part in perpetuating class inequalities in the welfare field.'

(Foster 1983: xi–xii)

Some kind of regulation, either of the conditions of access to services or of the recipients themselves, is an integral part of each of the various forms of social-service provision.

However, the point to notice here is not so much that the forms of regulation may have significant distributive consequences. Rather, it is that the analysis of social-policy instruments in terms of their distributive consequences alone will always be incomplete. Feminists have argued, for example, that the forms of welfare provision tend to privilege certain patterns of domestic relationships between adults and between adults and children. Or again, it is frequently argued that the receipt of means-tested benefits is likely to be experienced as degrading. We consider some of these issues in later chapters.

But if social-policy provision generally involves regulation of the conditions of access or of the recipients themselves, what remains of the equality of status that Marshall presents as the basis of the social component of citizenship? The problem is particularly acute in the case of means-tested benefits or when welfare professionals exercise discretionary control over their clients' access to services. Means tests are often regarded as humiliating and stigmatizing. There are numerous studies showing that the presence of a means test discourages the use of services by the poor (e.g. Townsend 1979). But there is a different point to notice here, namely, that the means-tested provision of goods and services requires that their recipients be subjected to a scrutiny that precisely differentiates them from the majority of other citizens. Even in the case of services that are not means tested or formally selective, like the general practitioner or hospital sectors of the NHS, receptionists and professionals themselves clearly regulate access to their services. My point here is not to argue against regulation – far from it – but rather to indicate the problems posed by the forms of policy provision for the analysis of post-war social policy in terms of Marshall's notion of citizenship. The claim that British social policy underlies a broad equality of status could be advanced only at the cost of ignoring the organizational forms in which its goods and services are provided.

IV

Citizenship and inflation

The last two chapters considered a view of British society that was widely shared by politicians, academics, and civil servants involved with social policy throughout much of the post-war period. This view is now generally regarded as unsatisfactory, even by its one-time proponents. The economic-policy failures of successive British governments during the 1960s and 1970s have done much to under-mine Crosland's optimistic picture of the capacity of government to manage the economy. We can no longer rely on economic growth to finance a politics of painless redistribution through public expenditure on services. The new economic climate therefore implies that social policies aimed at promoting Marshall's equality of citizenship or at the eradication of poverty can no longer rely on broad electoral support, or even apathy. Donnison therefore argues in 'Social Policy since Titmuss' (1979) for a reappraisal of the assumptions of the consensus view. In particular, he suggests, we should pay more attention to the economic and political settings of social policy, and to the links between the welfare and other sectors.

With the collapse of the old consensus we have also seen the emergence or re-emergence of alternative assessments of the welfare state, some of which will be discussed towards the end of this book. But first we consider two further sets of problems for the consensus view. The first is the argument that the supposed changes in British society invoked in support of the consensus view have potentially destructive consequences in the longer term. Two strands of this argument are particularly important here. One, considered in this chapter, is that citizenship and economic growth lead to the emer-gence of a mature working class willing and able to use its strength to secure inflationary increases in real wages. The other, considered in Chapter V, is that political democracy and the belief in the capacities of government intervention lead both to government over-load and to increasing demands on the productive capacity of the economy. The second set of arguments are that public expenditure on social services has markedly inegalitarian consequences. The evidence here is generally unambiguous and is surveyed in books by Halsey, Field, Townsend, and le Grand. Consideration of these authors' attempts at explanation will lead into a discussion of prob-lems in the use of social principles (such as equality) in the assess-ment of policies and social conditions.

CITIZENSHIP AND THE WORKING CLASS

The argument that citizenship and economic development lead in-exorably to the emergence of a mature working class, and thence to inflationary pressures, is most clearly presented in John Goldthorpe's influential contribution, 'The Current Inflation', *The Political Economy of Inflation* (Hirsch and Goldthorpe 1978). In effect, Goldthorpe takes up Marshall's argument about citizenship and social class, and develops it in a slightly different direction. We have seen that Mar-shall analyses British society in terms of a compromise between conflicting principles of citizenship and class. He also suggests, without developing the point, that this 'phase will not continue indefinitely' (Marshall 1950: 84). Goldthorpe departs from Marshall in his insistence on the dynamic character of class relations. He agrees that citizenship conflicts with the class system, and goes on to suggest that the development of the working class will inevitably undermine any compromise between them. In this argument, inflation is an effect of the co-existence in a society of the conflicting principles of citizenship, on the one side, and the market, on the other. Since both operate in the more prosperous societies of the capitalist West, we should expect similar problems to develop in these societies.

Goldthorpe's article begins by identifying significant elements in economists' accounts of inflation that are 'residual', in the sense that they don't fit in the analytical schemas of economics. For example, monetarist accounts of inflation as a consequence of mone-tary expansion pose the question of why governments fail to restrain that expansion. In so far as monetarism offers an explanation, it is usually couched in terms of the workings of a 'political market', in which interest-group pressures and electoral considerations lead to policies which increase the rate of money creation. Such explanations are notoriously inadequate (Tomlinson 1981; Toye 1976), and Goldthorpe notes that they open up properly sociological questions regarding the conditions of group formation and action. He makes similar points in relation to other economic theories of inflation. What the resort to residual categories shows here is that sociology really does have something to offer, that economists' and sociologists' accounts of inflation are complementary. However, that modest beginning masks a far grander enterprise. When we proceed to treat these 'residual' elements in terms of the mainstream sociological tradition it turns out that inflation (like other social phenomena) is really grounded in social structure. In this case, it is grounded in market relations which function as a

'source of social divisions and antagonisms which may then lie at the root of what are experienced as economic problems. Hence comes the supposition which must be basic to sociological enquiry into any such problem, inflation of course included: namely, that the economic problem is to an important degree epiphenomenal.'
(Goldthorpe 1978: 212)

In fact, we shall see that the economic problem here is rendered epiphenomenal only by means of a striking sociological reductionism.

Goldthorpe's approach is to locate the inflation of the 1970s in the context of longer-term changes in forms of stratification. Precisely because it is a system of inequality, stratification will resist egalitarian change.

'But if . . . such a change is brought about, then the nature of a stratification "system" also gives rise to the likelihood of their being, so to speak, a burst of "positive feedback", amplifying the change that has occurred – and, of course, threatening ultimately to disrupt the system, unless either its self-sustaining properties reassert themselves or external influences of a countervailing kind come into play.'

(*ibid*.: 196)

Egalitarian changes introduce destabilizing tensions to stratification systems. They must be corrected or they will undermine the system. In relation to the British class system Goldthorpe notes three processes tending to increase such tensions: the decay of the status order; the realization of citizenship; and the emergence of a 'mature' working class.

THE DECAY OF THE STATUS ORDER

On the first point, Goldthorpe introduces a modified form of Marshall's distinction between two kinds of class system. The modern system of class inequalities is 'essentially *de facto*', and from any moral standpoint largely arbitrary: 'Status inequalities, on the other hand, are an aspect of "socially constructed reality": they imply some measure of cognitive and evaluative consensus on the attributes indicative of social worth and superiority' (*ibid.*: 198). On this account a status order is, by definition, one that is accepted. It follows that if class inequalities correlate with those of a status order, they are able to derive from the consensual nature of this order a normative basis' (*ibid.*: 198).

What has happened in Britain and other capitalist societies is that the old, established status-order has been progressively undermined by the development and functioning of the market economy. The cash nexus has taken hold in all areas of social life; urbanization and geographical mobility have undermined local status-orders, and generalized notions of social worth have broken down. The result is that 'class inequalities come increasingly to be seen, and to be judged, for what they are – the products of the market economy – without the benefit of the normative camouflage which the status order previously created' (*ibid.*: 200). In this argument, Goldthorpe makes a traditional sociological move in presenting modernization as a process in which the market displaces an essentially moral order of society. In this case we are asked to imagine that there was once (it is not clear when) a kind of Merrie England in which everyone both knew their place and accepted it. The destruction of this imagined order by the market has resulted in a new level of dissent and conflict, reflecting a 'more rational appreciation of the nature of class inequalities' (*ibid.*: 201).

THE REALIZATION OF CITIZENSHIP

Secondly, there is the realization of citizenship, whose development Goldthorpe presents in roughly Marshall's terms. The implications of citizenship for the system of class inequalities are ambiguous. On the one hand, the existence of a common set of civil, political, and social rights allows some differences to be legitimized on meritocratic grounds. On the other hand, there is a problematic contrast between the principled equality of citizenship rights and the unprincipled inequalities of the market. The 'logic of citizenship' points to the further development of citizenship rights in the sphere of production. In particular, Goldthorpe's paper argues that the use of unemployment as an instrument of policy runs counter to 'the principle of citizenship, and, in particular, to the current tendency towards an expansion of rights within the sphere of work' (*ibid.*: 204).

THE DEVELOPMENT OF THE WORKING CLASS

These two processes threaten the class inequalities of the market system, but, Goldthorpe argues, their full impact will be felt 'only as a working class develops whose members have grown up entirely under the new conditions that have been created' (*ibid.*: 205). In this respect, Britain must be regarded as showing 'the leading edge . . . of a generally emergent phenomenon' (*ibid.*: 205). There are two respects in which the development of an industrial society tends to create a mature working class. One is demographic. The working class becomes increasingly self-recruiting, first with the decline of the agricultural sector and the traditional petty-bourgeoisie, and secondly, with the expansion of the new middle classes. The latter effectively reduces the chances of downwards mobility into the working class. On the first point, especially, Britain is some way ahead of other advanced capitalist societies. The members of its working class have a 'relatively high degree of homogeneity in their social backgrounds and patterns of life experience' (*ibid.*: 206).

The other respect in which the British working class is mature is socio-political. Over several generations in a relatively stable national community the working class has been able to build up its economic and political capacities through the development of trades unions and other organizations. In this respect Britain has been distinctive among the larger West European societies in having long-established civil and political rights, and comparative political stability over a long period. In the absence of war or major political convulsions, a similarly mature working class must be expected to develop in other Western societies. What has happened in Britain therefore

> 'points to the outcome that is most logically to be expected so far as the socio-political character of the working class is concerned, from the prolonged association of a developing capitalist economy and a stable 'liberal-pluralist' or 'social' democracy.'
>
> (*ibid.*: 207)

On the one hand, the British working class has a high degree of demographic homogeneity and a well-developed organizational capacity for action. On the other hand, the decay of the status order and the realization of citizenship mean that the working class lacks any value commitment to the inequalities generated by the operation of market forces. This account of the formation of a mature working class has some similarities to Marxist notions of the development of the proletariat into a class-conscious political unity. However, there is no suggestion in Goldthorpe's argument that a mature working class will aim at the revolutionary overthrow of capitalism. The formation of a mature working class results in a distributional struggle in which the efforts of organized labour to maintain or improve real wages generates an inexorable pressure towards inflation. The problem for governments is therefore to cope not only with inflation itself, but also and more seriously with the structural conflicts that lie behind it and the danger that 'an increasingly delegitimated structure of class inequality will prove no longer capable of institutional containment' (*ibid.*: 208). In the short term, inflation may have a positive advantage for governments, since it allows the distributional struggle to proceed in money terms while reducing its real income effects. In the longer term, however, governments in the capitalist democracies will have to confront the problems posed by a mature and powerful working class that, without being especially revolutionary, is unwilling to put up with the outcomes of the market system. Governments should be expected to favour incomes policies as a means of combating inflation precisely because they require some accommodation to be reached with the working class and its organizations; that is, they involve a measure of working-class integration which the market system alone does not. The danger of a monetarist approach is that it might provoke a reaction from organized labour, with 'the crisis of legitimacy now existing in the sphere of distribution being extended into that of political authority also' (*ibid.*: 209).

POLITICS AND SOCIOLOGICAL REDUCTIONISM

What Goldthorpe appears to offer is an account of the British inflation of the 1970s that overcomes the limitations of the economists' explanations by locating their 'residual' categories in the context of an underlying social structure 'so that what was previously treated as error, ignorance or unreason can be seen as a response by actors which is in accord with the logic of their situation' (*ibid.*: 211). Where economists and others have been concerned with the inflationary consequences of high levels of employment, Goldthorpe locates the source of the pressure on wages in the delegitimation of class differences, the normative basis of full-employment policy in the growth of citizenship, and the organizational strength of the working class in its demographic and socio-political maturity.

Perhaps, in 1978, that approach might have seemed plausible, but subsequent events have not been kind to Goldthorpe's argument. Governments have not been prevented from using unemployment as an instrument of policy by citizenship and the normative appeal of the 'right to work'. Monetarist policies have provoked some reaction from organized labour and from Labour local authorities. But that reaction has had limited popular support even within the working class. It would be an exaggeration to talk of a crisis of legitimacy in the sphere of political authority – except perhaps in some inner-city areas. There are indeed serious problems with Goldthorpe's argument, but, as we saw with Crosland, reference to subsequent events is not enough to tell us what those problems are. The following discussion is intended to identify some of the weaknesses in Goldthorpe's analysis and to show, in particular, that some of its problems derive from its use of Marshall's categories and others derive from a socio-logical reductionism.

THE TIMELESSNESS OF 'THE CURRENT INFLATION'

We may begin by asking what Goldthorpe's argument has to tell us about British society in the 1970s. The answer, unfortunately, is not very much. Although the title of Goldthorpe's paper refers to the 'current inflation', the currency of the 1970s plays no significant part in his argument. In particular, there is nothing to indicate why the 'current inflation' should have occurred when it did, why it should not have occurred, say, ten or fifteen years earlier. In itself this is not too much of a problem for Goldthorpe's account, since it is always possible to allow economic factors a limited role in triggering an inflationary expression of the underlying social tensions. But the timeless character of the argument is itself an index of more serious problems.

We have already noted a related index in the supposed decay of the status order, starting from some unspecified point in the past. If that decay is itself the source of a new level of dissent and tension, then it would seem that the level of social tension must have been lower at earlier stages in the process of decay. The identification of any specific starting point in British history as a period of harmony and consensus would have seemed somewhat implausible. Perhaps there were other sources of tension in the past which have themselves decayed along with the status order? But in that case there would be no reason to expect an increase in tension with the decay of status. To put the point another way, the decay of the status order can appear as a plausible source of social tension only if the status order itself is given no clear temporal location.

THE MATURITY OF THE WORKING CLASS?

Now consider the maturity of the British working class. What this amounts to in Goldthorpe's argument is the following. First, there is limited movement into the British working class from elsewhere, so that a clear majority of the working class are themselves born of working class parents. Goldthorpe presents that as entailing a homogeneity of social backgrounds and life experiences. Secondly, British working-class institutions have been able to develop throughout a long period of relative social and political stability. In that respect Britain is said to be ahead of the rest of the advanced capitalist world. We should expext similar levels of tension to develop in the other large capitalist democracies as their working classes mature.

There are several problems here. First, there is the question of the contribution of class analysis to our understanding of politics, which we consider in Chapter VII. Secondly, Goldthorpe's argument suggests that the ony important differences between the organized working class in Britain and in other capitalist democracies are to do with how long they have been able to develop without major demographic or political disturbances. What matters is the cultural homogeneity of the working class and the age of its institutions. For the rest, the particular organizational character of the British labour movement and the structure of collective bargaining (compared, say, with Sweden, or West Germany, or Japan) has no bearing on British inflation or its relatively low rate of growth of productivity. This argument, too, is hardly plausible. It is not necessarily a matter of placing the blame on British trades unions to suggest that the specific institutional forms of the labour movement and collective bargaining have some bearing on Britain's economic problems.

Again, Goldthorpe's use of the metaphor of maturity suggests that the labour movement in Britain is better placed to look after the interests of its members than its equivalents in countries with a less 'mature' working class. That implication is debatable, to say the least. It would be difficult to argue, for example, that the labour movement in Britain has done a better job of looking after the interests of the working class than those in Austria or West Germany – both countries where the working class is significantly less mature in both of Goldthorpe's senses. Indeed, Robert Taylor's discussion of the effectiveness of the British trades unions concludes as follows: 'By the standards of the countries of the industrialised West, British unions have so far failed to exercise constructive, let alone radical power and influence' (Taylor 1980: 291). It might perhaps be objected that the standards to which Taylor refers are not themselves an appropriate test of working-class maturity. That may be. But it is not necessary to agree with Taylor's conclusions to see the problem they pose for Goldthorpe's argument; namely, that his claims regarding the socio-political *maturity* of the British working class are open to considerable dispute. Here, too, Goldthorpe's discussion suggests that the specific institutional forms of the British labour movement have no bearing on its effectiveness – except in so far as they may be regarded as a simple function of the time they have had to develop.

In these two respects Goldthorpe's account of the development of a mature working class as a simple consequence of citizenship and capitalist development must be regarded as highly problematic. A footnote denies that this process is inevitable and suggests that there may be countervailing tendencies to maturation. The example he gives is that of immigrant workers reducing the demographic homogeneity of the working class. Politics plays no part in the maturation process except in so far as it disrupts its historical continuity; for example, through the impact of war or dictatorship. In effect, Goldthorpe presents a convergence thesis for capitalist democracies: in the absence of severe disruption they must all be expected to develop in the direction of contemporary Britain.

This effective relegation of the significance of politics in the development of the capitalist democracies is more than a little surprising in view of Goldthorpe's own powerful argument against an earlier convergence thesis. In his 'Social Stratification in Industrial Society' (1962) he argues agains the view that industrialization will in itself bring about a convergence between the stratification systems of East and West, and he does so by reference to significant differences in the politics of those societies. Indeed, Goldthorpe returns to that point in a more recent paper when he concludes that:

'Western capitalist societies have moved in divergent directions in their responses to economic problems and further that, in consequence, they now face different sets of political choices. . . . Which alternatives will be pursued . . . will be determined only by the future course of political action in particular nations.'

(Goldthorpe 1984: 340)

The idea that all that is needed for working-class maturation is economic development and the civil and political liberties of capitalist democracy is by no means peculiar to Goldthorpe's argument. A similar account of the socio-political development of the working class was given by Kautsky in his commentary on the Erfurt Programme of the German Social Democratic Party towards the end of the nineteenth century (Kautsky 1971). Kautsky wrote as a Marxist, and his expectations of the political maturity of the working class were rather different from Goldthorpe's. Nevertheless, they share the view that the political maturity of the working class is only a matter of time, given capitalist economic development and relatively stable political democracy.

Kautsky's arguments, of course, have long since been discredited, not only by the tendentious polemics of Lenin and others of his political opponents, but also by the manifest failure of the working class in any capitalist democracy to develop as he suggested. But here again we should be wary of allowing allusion to the vagaries of history to substitute for critical analysis. Goldthorpe and Kautsky may assign different contents to the concept of the maturity of the working class, and so too do the Marxist advocates of a democratic road to socialism, but their arguments suffer a similar fundamental weakness (see Hindess 1983). In effect, they assume that the unity of the working class as a social and political force is given as a consequence of the positions of its members in the organization of capitalist production. Of course, Goldthorpe, like Kautsky and many others before him, acknowledges the presence of sectional divisions, but these are conceived as divisions within a preconceived unity. It is in this sense that Goldthorpe can refer, for example, to 'the working class and its organisations' (Goldthorpe 1978: 208). If that unity is conceived as given in the nature of capitalist production, then the only significant role of politics must lie in furthering or inhibiting the practical expression of that unity.

SOCIOLOGICAL REDUCTIONISM

What is at stake in the timeless quality of these arguments and in the attempt to derive political and economic consequences from the maturity of the working class, is a sociological reductionism which renders significant elements of politics invisible, or at any rate insignificant, for the purposes of the argument. In this respect Goldthorpe's class analysis shares many of the problems of the Marxist positions which we consider in Chapter VII. His analysis of the social conditions underlying the British inflation of the 1970s pays no attention to the conditions and organizations of political and economic conflict in Britain – save for noting that the latter have been able to develop over a relatively long period. The effect is to ignore the political parties, trades unions, and employers' associations, state agencies, and other bodies that constitute the principal arenas and agencies of political and economic struggle. It is also to ignore the ideologies and forms of political and economic calculation in terms of which those struggles are conducted and supporters are mobilized around them. Once the specific features of British political life, with the exception of its relatively stable democratic character, are discounted in this way, there can be no great difficulty in discounting the effects of differences in the political life of Britain and others of the capitalist democracies. Once that has been achieved, it is an easy matter to present Britain as exhibiting 'the leading . . . edge of a generally emergent phenomenon' (*ibid.*: 205).

PRINCIPLES AND SOCIAL CONDITIONS

We have just noted a striking sociological reductionism in the derivation of political and economic consequences from the maturity of the working class without reference to the specific forms and conditions of political and economic conflict in British society. The conditions responsible for the inflation of the 1970s are effectively reduced to a combination of a capitalist market economy, on the one hand, with significant normative elements which threaten to undermine it, on the other. The crucial features of the latter are the realization of the principle of citizenship and the removal of the normative camouflage of class inequalities with the decay of the status order. Citizenship poses a problem for a market economy as a result of the contrast between the principled equality of rights in the political sphere and the unprincipled inequalities of the market. In that respect the principles inherent in citizenship generate further challenges to the *status quo*. Goldthorpe comments that 'the further working out of the logic of citizenship . . . is in the direction of reinforcing and extending citizenship rights specifically in the sphere of production' (*ibid.*: 203). Or again, we are told that workers' expectations with regard to the maintenance of relatively full employment 'now [1978] have a normative and not merely an empirical grounding – as ones relating to rights and not just probabilities' (*ibid.*: 203).

In effect, this part of Goldthorpe's argument reproduces Marshall's account of the tensions inherent in the co-existence of the conflicting principles of citizenship and the market. We may or may not agree that further extensive democratization in the sphere of employment is desirable. But apart from a small minority of left-wing intellectuals and political activists, the British labour movement has shown little sign of concern with this issue in recent years. The point here is that Goldthorpe's argument, and the rather different arguments of Marshall and Titmuss, present the realization of a principle in some spheres of a society and its non-realization elsewhere in that same society, as a source of social tension.

Why should principles be regarded as a source of social tension in this way? There is more at stake here than the banal suggestion that people committed to different principles are likely to disagree with each other. These arguments presuppose the legitimacy of analysing social conditions as the more or less consistent expression or realization of principles – so that, for example, the institutional conditions of parliamentary democracy express, *inter alia*, the principle of equality, while those of capitalist production deny that principle. If that mode of analysis is acceptable, then when two principles conflict or where one principle is imperfectly realized, we should indeed expect to find corresponding social conflicts. Conversely, as in Goldthorpe's imagined and now decayed status order in which class inequalities are the expression of a normative consensus, we should expect to find social harmony. What is at stake here is the question of how social principles or values relate to social conditions, and what part they could play in their analysis. We return to that question towards the end of this book.

V

The contradictions of collectivism

The last chapter considered one argument suggesting problems for the consensus view, to the effect that the growth of citizenship in a developed capitalist economy generates a level of distributional conflict leading to inflationary pressures. Considered as an account of the British inflation of the 1970s, Goldthorpe's argument suffers serious weaknesses, notably a striking sociological reductionism. Thus, while he insists that social antagonisms lie at the root of Britain's inflation, Goldthorpe pays not the slightest attention to the specific institutions, organizations, and ideologies which provide the conditions in which conflicts are conducted. We also noted, as a problem for later discussion, that a significant part of Goldthorpe's argument depends on the analysis of social conditions as the more or less consistent expression of principles.

The present chapter considers a more general argument to the effect that the consensus view is undermined by the very politics that follow from it. The argument can be found in several forms, some of them expressing little more than the traditional liberal reservations about government intervention in the economy and social life. We return to those reservations in Chapters VIII and IX. In its more general form, the argument presents both an explanation of the growth of government activity and an account of its consequences in terms of interest-group pressures. Demands on government policy develop inexorably under conditions of political democracy, once it is generally assumed that governments have both the capacity and the responsibility to manage the economy and to intervene more generally in the interests of social welfare. Sectional interests make demands, and political parties compete for their support with promises of action. The range of government policies and programmes therefore tends to expand in response to demands. On the other hand, once a programme is in place, it generates a set of interests in its maintenance among the groups whose interests it promotes and within the civil service. The growth of government intervention is therefore the result of demands from particular interest groups and of organizational inertia.

Why should the expansion of government social and economic intervention be regarded as problematic? Our main concern in this chapter is with analyses of government programmes in terms of interest-group behaviour, but it is worth commenting first on the suggestion that the development of big government itself involves a loss of effectiveness. In *Understanding Big Government* Rose (1984) identifies four major arguments of this kind. The first is that the growth of government increases the demands it makes on society's resources, ultimately to the detriment of other potential uses of those resources. Secondly, there is the claim that the growth in size and complexity of government organization generates inefficiency. Thirdly, there is the suggestion that government will be tempted into policy areas in which it has no effective means of action and no clear measures of its effectiveness. Programmes aimed at the abolition of poverty or crime are often cited in this connection. Finally, there is the view that the increase in the number and range of programmes will lead to contradictions between the programmes themselves.

In fact, Rose's discussion of big government in the major advanced Western societies suggests that three of these problems have not arisen.

'The growth of government has not caused a great reduction in organisational effectiveness, or contradictions between programmes; nor has it meant the proliferation of ineffective programmes based upon soft technologies. The programmes that have grown most are welfare state programmes which tend to retain their effectiveness with growth.'

Rose (1984: 215)

There remains the first problem, that of paying for its costs. Arguments concerning the excessive costs of big government usually concentrate on one or both of two issues. First, it has been suggested that the expansion of government programmes leads to it making excessive demands on the productive resources of the economy. In the British context that argument was advanced in an influential book by Bacon and Eltis, *Britain's Economic Problem: Too Few Producers* (1976), and in a Marxist version by Glyn and Sutcliffe, *British Capitalism: Workers and the Profits Squeeze* (1972). These books are not without interest, but in both cases the general argument is vitiated by the assumption that goods and services not produced as commodities (e.g. in education or the NHS) make no productive contribution to society. This results in the treatment of many government pro- grammes as essentially unproductive; that is, as a drain on society's resources. There are, of course, some public services of this kind; for example, the provision of care for the elderly, the terminally ill, and the chronically disabled, most of whom can be expected to make little further positive contribution to economic activity. If the provision of public services depended mainly on an expectation of economic return, then these services would have to go. For the rest, it is difficult to defend the claim that the overall effect of free public education and medical services is to reduce the productive capacity of society (George and Wilding 1984). There may indeed be problems over the financing of public expenditure, but the analysis is not helped by the suggestion that services that are not marketed offer no productive return.

The other issue concerns the level and rate of increase of taxation. This can have a significant effect on personal disposable incomes, especially in periods of relatively low economic growth. In America and the major European economies the costs of government pro- grammes have grown faster than the economy as a whole, and personal incomes after tax have grown more slowly (Rose 1984: 220). This is said to pose problems for governments because of the growth of tax evasion and political resistance to taxation and to some of the programmes it finances. Heclo suggests, for example, that one effect of financing the post-war expansion of social-welfare expenditure out of the increment of growth has been to 'devalue the political commitment necessary to sustain social policy' (Heclo 1981: 397). We discussed this issue briefly towards the end of Chapter II.

Turning now to the supposed effects of interest-group behaviour, two lines of argument have been advanced to show why the politics that follows from the consensus view is ultimately self-destructive.

One concerns the price that governments feel they have to pay in order to secure the co-operation of various interest groups. The other concerns the effects of the pursuit of advantage by a large number of distinct interest groups. This second line of argument has an influential pedigree in rational-choice theory and its applications to the analysis of national politics; notably, in rather different forms, in Olson's *The Rise and Decline of Nations* (1982) and Thurow's *The Zero-Sum Society* (1981). The argument is that concentrated and more or less well-organized groups use their power to exact privileges from the state and to block anything that threatens to damage their interests. This results in what some liberal authors have called a 'new Hobbesian dilemma', a self-defeating war of all against all through the indirect medium of government action.

These two lines of argument have been brought together in Beer's *Britain Against Itself: The Political Contradictions of Collectivism* (1982), and it is his discussion that we concentrate on here, returning below to the 'new Hobbesian dilemma' and rational-choice arguments. Beer's book is an ambitious and wide-ranging account of contemporary British politics, and there is more to his arguments than the points we consider in this discussion. He defines the collectivist polity in terms of 'the programs of the managed economy and the welfare state and also the political parties and pressure groups which have shaped those programs and in turn have been shaped by them' (Beer 1982: 10). In this sense collectivism is a political system based on the consensus view which we considered in the first part of this book. It involved a commitment by the major parties to 'government intervention in and responsibility for the economic and social order as a whole' (*ibid.*: 11). Beer notes that the Conservative Party was committed to this position by the late 1940s. He cites, for example, the 1950 election manifesto with its many specific pledges 'regarding the health service, pensions, education, housing, the farm program, and, above all, "full employment as the first aim of a Conservative Government" ' (*ibid.*: 7). Beer claims, as I have done, that this conception of government responsibility was common ground between the leaderships of two major parties until recently. He goes on to argue that collectivist politics undermines the power of government for two major reasons; first, because of the price government has to pay to secure the co-operation of various interest groups, and secondly, because of what he calls 'pluralistic stagnation'. We consider these reasons in a moment, but before proceeding it is important to notice that Beer presents them as part of a larger and more complex argument. In his view, the processes of pluralistic stagnation are themselves predicated on the decline of a hierarchical and deferential civic culture which had previously held pluralistic tendencies in check. We will return to this point.

THE PROBLEM OF CONSENT

In the capitalist and more or less democratic societies of the modern West significant areas of social and economic activity are not within the direct control of government. The effectiveness of government policies relating to these areas therefore depends in part on the co-operation or at least the consent of others. Beer suggests that as the range of government interventions expands, so too will the range of groups and interests whose co-operation is required, with the result that government capacity to achieve its policy objectives will diminish. In order to see what is at stake in this suggestion, let us begin by returning to Crosland's account of government's capacity for economic management.

Government and business

An important part of Crosland's argument concerning the transformation of capitalism is the claim that the major levers of economic power are now in the hands of government. British governments now have all the powers they need to regulate the overall performance of the economy. Within broad limits, they can determine the balance between consumption and investment, the post-tax distribution of income, and so on. As for the performance of specific industries, we have seen Crosland claim that 'there is now no insuperable economic difficulty about the government imposing its will, provided it has one, on either private or public industry' (Crosland 1956: 468). On this view, the obstacles to government economic management are essentially a matter of political will rather than a matter of the means of action at the disposal of governments and their limitations. We have noted some of the consequences of Crosland's failure to recognize the importance of considering government policy in relation to the specific instruments at its disposal. We must now turn to a related problem.

How is government to impose its will on the performance of public or private industry? Governments have a variety of instruments at their disposal: the tax system and general legislation, the offer of diverse grants and other inducements, the use of its own purchasing policy, and so on. But, with the exception of nationalized industries, any government must use these instruments to affect the performance of economic agents that are not within its direct control. Government economic management has therefore to be concerned with the aggregate behaviour of legally autonomous economic agents. In effect, capitalist enterprises are subject to such requirements as may be specified in legislation, but they cannot otherwise be compelled to act as governments desire. Indeed, even where requirements are specified in, say, health and safety or equal employment legislation, there is clearly no guarantee of compliance. For the rest, governments can attempt to modify the macro-economic climate within which enterprises reach their decisions, and it can wave sticks and carrots in front of particular firms or sectors of industry. In different ways the monetarist policies of the Thatcher governments and the 'Keynesian' policies that preceded them, are based on the hope that the combination of climate, threat and promise will induce enterprises to behave appropriately. Unfortunately, much as British governments may wish to increase the level of manufacturing investment, there is no way that private firms can be made to invest in accordance with those wishes. The obstacles to government imposing its will, even if it has one, are more substantial than Crosland was prepared to admit.

The limitations on government capacity to control the behaviour of private enterprises have been widely recognized on the left. In the late 1960s and throughout the 1970s, for example, it was commonplace on the left of the Labour Party to argue that Labour government policies for industry and economic growth had been frustrated by 'investment strikes'; that is, by the failure of senior management in large private companies and financial institutions to invest as government plans required. The strike metaphor has the advantage of forcefully suggesting that part of the blame for Britain's industrial decline should be placed on the side of the owners. The disadvantage is that it suggests a degree of co-ordination on the part of employers and financial institutions which is hardly plausible in the British context. Companies have good reasons for not taking government economic projections as a reliable basis for their investment decisions. There is no need to invoke a co-ordinated plan to frustrate government policies to explain their failures to make the desired investments.

It was partly to overcome this perceived limitation that *Labour's Programme, 1973* introduced proposals for a National Enterprise Board and for Planning Agreements (renamed Agreed Development Plans in *Labour's Programme, 1982*). Under the Planning Agreement system the government would secure information from the larger companies concerning their plans for investment, product development, and related issues. The idea was to provide a means of making large enterprises 'accountable for their behaviour, and for bringing into line those which refuse to comply – using where necessary the extensive powers under the proposed Industry Act'. The *Programme* noted that threats and promises had not proved sufficient to bring the level of national investment under government control and argued that 'only direct control, through ownership, of a substantial and vital sector of the growth industries. . . . will allow a Labour Government of the future to achieve its essential planning objectives in the national interest' (Labour Party 1973: 18). The difficulty with this argument, of course, is that it depends on the capacity of government to make a reasonable job of managing the performance of the public sector, which is far from ensured by the mere fact of public ownership. Indeed, some of the most disastrous investment decisions in post-war British history have been taken under government control (Concorde, the 'modernization' of the renationalized steel industry in the late 1960s, the much-vaunted Plan for Coal, etc.).

Returning to the general argument, Crosland is right to insist that there has been a considerable expansion of the means of economic intervention available to governments. But he is wrong to claim that governments are thereby enabled to impose their will either on the behaviour of the economy as a whole or on that of particular industries or sectors. Post-war governments have a significantly different, and in some respects greater, capacity for economic management than their pre-war counterparts, but they have still to operate with and through the institutions of a largely private-enterprise economy. This means that the effectiveness of government policy frequently depends on the performance of private economic agents.

Now, consider Lindblom's discussion of this point in 'The Privileged Position of Business', Chapter 13 of his *Politics and Markets* (1977). In a predominantly private-enterprise economy, Lindblom argues, significant areas of public decision-making are removed from effective government control. Governments are concerned with the performance of business, but although they 'can forbid certain kinds of activity, they cannot command business to perform. They must induce rather than command' (Lindblom 1977: 173). Business performs functions which, in general, governments regard as indispensable. Lindblom therefore suggests that there is a continuous mutual adjustment between government and business, with sectors of industry or large companies offering performance in exchange for favours, and in some cases, the effective grant of governmental authority to businessmen. The dependence of government economic policy on the performance of the private sector is an inevitable feature of private-enterprise systems. The result is that 'a great degree of business control, unmatched by similar control exercised by any other group of citizens, comes to be exercised over government' (*ibid.*: 187). In Lindblom's view this privileged position may be reinforced by the activities of organized interest groups, but it is, in the first instance, a function of the desire of governments to coax business, given their limited ability to coerce it, into the appropriate performance. The striking ability of British governments, Labour and Conservative, to alienate business opinion indicates that the notion of 'business control' here rather overstates the case. Like the notion of 'investment strike', it suggests a degree of co-ordination on the part of business opinion that is implausible, however much governments might sometimes desire it. Lindblom is right to insist that governments have a rather different relation to business than to other more or less organized interests, and there are certainly cases where government policy is effectively controlled by business interests. But such control, when and where it exists, is not an inevitable consequence of the dependence of government on business performance.

Incomes policies

As a second example of the dependence of government interventions on outside agencies, consider the case of incomes policies. Government attempts to control the level of wage increases require either the use of unemployment and other devices to weaken the bargaining position of unions or else some kind of formal or informal accommodation with powerful unions. We have seen that Goldthorpe advocates the latter both as a means of controlling inflation and, more importantly, as a means of incorporating the working class and its organizations, thereby reducing the social tensions inherent in the operations of the market system. In order to reach such an accommodation it is necessary for government to offer something to the unions in return for their co-operation. In effect, control of wage increases by means of union co-operation involves giving the unions some control over government policies in other areas.

This implication is taken up by Brittan in his case against incomes policies (Brittan 1977). Part of his argument is that incomes policies are not effective means of combating inflation in the long run. But his more serious concern is with what he regards as the political consequences of adopting them. The problem is that what unions ask for in return for wage restraint has distorting effects on markets:

> 'incomes policy tends to be backed by a whole series of actions – from pressures on the nationalized industries to keep their prices artificially low, to dividend and price control, and punitive taxation of higher incomes and profits – which are inimical to the efficient working of a market economy and which, pushed too far, are also a threat to personal liberty.'
>
> (Brittan 1977: 13)

There are two points to Brittan's complaint. The first is that incomes policies interfere with the workings of markets. We return to that issue in the last two chapters of this book. The second point is that they encourage people to look to the political process for their well-being rather than to their own economic activity. These 'policies cause political conflict to enter into every nook and cranny of personal and business life' (*ibid.*: 13). From this point of view the great advantage of governments restricting themselves to monetary and fiscal policies in their battles against inflation 'is at bottom political. It does not involve asking the unions not to use the powers that they have; nor does it involve giving them extra power in the political arena' (*ibid.*: 13).

Here it is the political ambition of government to directly control the level of wage increases that brings political problems in its trail. Brittan's argument is part of a more general liberal case for limiting the powers and ambitions of government which I discuss in Chapter VIII. In the absence of that particular liberal commitment, of course, there is no reason in general to object to political interventions in the operations of markets. Nor is there any reason to suppose that the granting of powers to unions and other non-governmental agencies in return for their co-operation is necessarily to be deplored. But it is important to recognize the general point that here, as elsewhere, the effectiveness of government policies depends in part on the consent and co-operation of others.

This last comment returns us to Beer's argument. The paradox of government power in a free society is that 'the enormous new powers that government exercises over producer and consumer groups at the same time puts these groups in a position to frustrate those powers by refusing their cooperation and consent.' (Beer 1982: 14).

In fact, although Beer concentrates on the necessity of extra-governmental consent and co-operation, much the same point could be made about the senior civil service, public-sector corporations and local government. Labour ministers and ex-ministers have often complained of the effects of civil-service opposition. Richard Crossman, Barbara Castle and Tony Benn have all given examples from their experience as ministers, not just of foot-dragging, but also of civil servants actively campaigning against their ministers. Conservative ministers have sometimes faced similar problems. Some of the Labour left and the present Tory government have drawn the conclusion that a more ruthless and determined ministerial style is necessary, forcing decisions through regardless of opposition. Paul Hirst and I have argued elsewhere that that conclusion is seriously misleading (Hindess and Hirst 1983; Hindess 1983). In the British political system governments have no choice but to work through a complex and relatively intractable state machine. In many cases, no doubt, they can impose their will, but at considerable administrative and political cost. In this sense, Hartley Shawcross's notorious slogan 'We are the masters now' embodies a dangerous illusion of power.

The general argument then is that government policies depend on the consent or co-operation of groups and agencies that are often outside its direct control.The successful implementation of government policy is not in general simply a matter of government imposing its will, as Crosland tended to insist. Governments do not and cannot have the capacities of the kind that Crosland suggests. By expanding their means of intervention into many areas of social and economic life, governments have also increased their dependence on the co-operation of others. Beer quotes with approval the conclusion of a senior civil servant that 'as Government intervention expands, the power of the Government actually diminishes; that is to say the ratio between the responsibilities the Government has taken on and its power to discharge those responsibilities becomes less favourable' (in Beer 1982: 14). But that is to overstate the case. It is certainly a mistake for Crosland to identify the extension of government's capacity for action with the ability to impose its will. It is equally a mistake to identify the ability of others to frustrate government policy with a real diminution of government capacities.

PLURALISTIC STAGNATION

The other significant feature of collectivist politics in Beer's argument concerns what he calls 'pluralistic stagnation'. The term acquires several meanings in the course of his discussion, but the main ones relate to a defensiveness and resistance to change on the part of various interest groups and to the sheer number of different interests that play a part in political life. These combine to make agreed and co-ordinated action difficult to achieve, resulting in a paralysis of public choice. The importance of interest groups here is a consequence of the broad consensus of collectivist politics. Having abandoned 'the battle of opposing social philosophies' (*ibid.*: 16) parties in the era of consensus attempt to maintain and expand their electoral appeal by competing for the support of particular interests:

'The most striking instance of this tendency, it has seemed to me, was that glossy product of Gaitskellite revisionism put out in 1958 and entitled *Your Personal Guide to the Future Labour Offers You.* Conveniently thumb-indexed with references to "Your Home", "Your Job", "Education", "Health", "Age Without Fear", it enabled tenants, workers, patients, pensioners, and other prospective beneficiaries of Labour's largesse to turn directly to the promises beamed to them in accordance with the findings of the new science of survey research.'

(*ibid.*: 16)

The danger is that parties will compete for the support of various interests 'with no other object than winning office' (*ibid.*: 16) thereby generating a competitive scramble for rewards between interest groups. Beer identifies three main kinds of scramble: for benefits, for pay, and for subsidies.

THE BENEFITS SCRAMBLE

The development of the British welfare state has produced a large number of social programmes aimed at specific groups of beneficiaries. Many of these beneficiary groups have organized pressure groups (Child Poverty Action Group, Age Concern, Shelter, and so on) or other agencies (building societies, amenity organization and consumer groups, insurance companies, motoring organizations, etc.) claiming to represent their interests and to speak on their behalf. Beer's argument is that the large number of groups generates an upward pressure on overall public spending on benefits:

'Because so many are making claims, the claim of no single group can make much difference to the level of public expenditure. Self-restraint by a particular group, therefore would bring no discernible benefit to it or to any other group, but on the contrary would penalize the self-denying group with a significant loss. Hence, even though the group may recognize the need for all participants to moderate their claims, it will be tempted to raise its own.'

(*ibid.*: 30–1)

The result is that expenditure on 'social programs was driven out of control by the benefits scramble' (*ibid.*: 63). The same kind of analysis is applied to the pay and subsidy scrambles. The argument is that while each group may be able to see the point of restraining the overall level of expenditure, there is no compelling reason for any one of them to moderate its own demands. In addition, there are too many interests involved for them to achieve moderation through agreement. The problem, in other words 'is not a lack of knowledge, but the structure of the situation' (*ibid.*: 31).

In itself, the plethora of demands would not be too much of a problem. Governments after all are elected to govern; that is, to make choices between competing possibilities and to act on them. The problem comes, then, not so much from the demands as from the pattern of party competition, with each competing for the support of consumer groups. The result is a bidding up of promises and an over-commitment of public resources to the provision of benefits to various interest groups.

THE PAY AND SUBSIDY SCRAMBLES

Beer invokes a similar 'structure of the situation' in his account of the pay and subsidy scrambles. In the inter-war period Britain had a relatively centralized system of collective bargaining, with pay and working conditions in important sectors of industry settled by industry-wide negotiations. By the time of the *Report of the Royal Commission on Trade Unions and Employers' Associations* (Donovan Report) in 1968, it had become highly decentralized in many industries. Pay and conditions were increasingly determined both by national bargaining and by the activities of powerful shop stewards' organizations in many plants. The large number of bargaining units meant that no one bargain would have a significant effect on the overall level of wages and therefore on inflation. Equally, there was no overall benefit in any one group holding back, only a loss to the group concerned.

'Neither stupidity nor radicalism but the pluralism of this fragmented structure propelled British trade unionists, against their express opinions, into the pay scramble that swept over the country in the late 1960s and continued with mounting disorder, only briefly remitted, through the following decade.'

(Beer 1982: 55)

If the hope for an incomes policy to contain inflation was destroyed by a pay scramble, then, Beer argues, that of an industrial policy to boost investment and productivity 'was defeated by the similar logic of the subsidy scramble' (*ibid*.: 63). The end result of a long period of government attempts to direct economic activity through the carrot of subsidy and tax concessions has been 'precisely the opposite of its goal. Aiming at greater efficiency, competitiveness, and economic growth, the subsidy strategy has encouraged inefficiency, complacency, and economic stagnation' (*ibid*.: 74). Here, too, we are told, the problem lies not in the motivations of industrialists but in the logic of the situation. 'The manager will "shout" for a subsidy even if he recognises the actual tendency of the subsidy policy to diminish the economic achievement of the whole and its respective parts' (*ibid*.: 75).

THE NEW HOBBESIAN DILEMMA

In Beer's discussion the 'logic of the situation' rests on a specific 'cultural foundation, viz., distrust. Conversely, it points to the restoration of trust as a condition that would halt the Hobbesian struggle and revive the aggregative capacities of the system' (*ibid*.: 211). We return to that 'cultural foundation' in a moment, but first it is worth noting that a similar 'logic of the situation' plays a central part in the argument of certain liberals against what they regard as the unlimited democracy of Britain and other modern Western societies. Gray identifies it as one of three main supports of Hayek's contention (which we consider in a later chapter) that the idea of a mixed economy, as a half-way house between freedom and total state control, is a chimera (Gray 1984a, 1984b).

The argument works as follows. Once it is assumed that the state has both the ability and the responsibility to manage economic and social life in the interests of welfare, then there need be no limit to the scope of state intervention. In a democratic society where groups are relatively free to organize, then the 'logic of the situation' generates a 'Hobbesian' process of competitive struggle between more or less organized groups in favour of state intervention to further their interests.

In Hobbes's own argument the 'warre' of all against all operates in a state of nature, a condition in which individuals are not constrained by law and custom. The absolute powers of the sovereign are therefore required as a means of ending this 'warre' in the general interest. The Hobbesian dilemma of liberal argument therefore differs from Hobbes's 'warre' in two important respects. First, the competitive struggle does not take place in a state of nature but rather under conditions of unlimited political democracy. Instead of direct confrontation it involves

> 'a largely hidden struggle conducted in the political arena through the exercise of overt and covert pressure on government, politicians, political parties and bureaucrats. Only in some instances is the ruthlessness of the struggle brought to general public attention, as when British miners or French farmers attempt to use quasi-military tactics to surround and suspend the operation of ports or power stations.'
>
> (Burton 1984: 98)

Secondly, of course, it is a struggle between groups rather than individuals. Sometimes the groups are relatively well organized, as with trades unions and professional associations, farmers, trade associations, and employers' organizations. Sometimes, as we saw in Beer's discussion of the 'benefits scramble', there are pressure groups claiming to represent them. Finally, there are groups, such as ratepayers or council tenants, that need not be organized at all but whose support parties try to enlist at election times. For each of these groups the costs to their members (in terms of increased taxation) of the government programmes they favour are small compared with the benefits they expect to receive. As we saw with Beer's analysis, there is no need to assume that the competing groups are purely self-interested or that they are unaware of the consequences of their actions. The 'logic of the situation' means that there is little overall benefit in any particular group holding back, and there is a certain loss to the group itself.

The result is first that increasing demands are made of government, and secondly, that the better-organized groups attempt to block any government action which they see as damaging their interests. The general level of taxation therefore tends to rise while the ability of governments to implement their programmes is frustrated by the resistance of organized interests. The 'new Hobbesian' process, then, generates inflationary pressures (due to excessive taxation), an expansion of government programmes and a decline in their effectiveness. The only way this process can be stopped is by the imposition of constitutional constraints which curtail the powers of governments to intervene in social and economic life. Hayek and Friedman have both proposed constitutional constraints of this kind on the powers of democratically elected governments.

IS THERE A 'LOGIC' OF THE SITUATION?

There are several problems with this liberal argument in favour of limited government. Some of these concern its empirical foundations and support, and others concern the notion of there being a 'logic' in the situation. First, we have seen that the liberal argument implies an inexorable tendency for the demands on government and the general level of taxation to increase (e.g. Buchanan *et al.* 1978). In fact, careful discussion of the evidence by Toye (1976) and Tomlinson (1981) has shown that applications of this approach in the fields of public expenditure and public finance are generally crude and ill informed, and that they provide little empirical support. The election of right-wing governments in Britain and the USA committed to reducing taxation and rolling back the state, however limited their successes, suggests that whatever tendencies there may be for a secular growth in levels of taxation are far from being inexorable. Indeed, one liberal critic has gone so far as to suggest that the 'Hobbesian' process develops its own limits (Barry 1984 – but see the criticisms in Gray 1984b and Burton 1984).

Secondly, the notion of 'unlimited government' is a curious one to apply to Britain, or indeed to any society of the modern West. In Britain, as in other parliamentary democracies, there are substantial constitutional and other limitations on the scope of democratic government: the independence of the judiciary, the institutions of common law, and following Britain's accession to the EEC, the European Court, the autonomy of the Central Bank, which in one way or another is characteristic of the advanced capitalist democracies, numerous powerful private interests, and so on. Modern Western governments do restrict the liberty of individuals, and they are sometimes right to do so. They are clearly not limited in quite the way many liberals would desire, but it requires a certain paranoia to suggest that they are unlimited.

Finally, there is the notion of there being a 'logic' given in the situation so that the outcome is a logical consequence of the structure of the situation itself. What this view requires is that the interests of each group are given by its position in the structure and that it acts rationally in pursuit of those interests. Notice first that Beer and the liberals argue for very different conclusions on the basis of that supposed 'logic'. Where the liberals conclude that there should be self-imposed restrictions on the powers of government in democratic societies, Beer argues for a 'restoration' of the trust which he believes existed in Britain under the 'civic culture'.

In fact, Beer's recourse to notions of 'trust' and 'civic culture' undermines the notion of there being a 'logic' given in the situation. The 'civic culture' in Beer's analysis

> 'consisted of attitudes toward political behaviour that were widely held at all levels of the polity. Embodying hierarchical and organic values, these attitudes strongly supported structures of action which mobilized consent for their respective goals among their constituents.'
>
> (Beer 1982: 209)

We need not go along with Beer's account of the civic culture or of its decline to see that his argument here relies on a further claim; namely, that the behaviour of individuals and groups depends, at least in part, on the attitudes and other ideas in terms of which they assess the conditions in which they find themselves.

In other words, their behaviour depends on the political ideologies, traditions, and other ideas which they employ in analysing their situation, and on the means of action available to them. Once that is accepted, as I think it must be, then the argument from the 'logic' of the situation must collapse (Hindess 1984). The trouble with analysing Britain's political and economic problems as consequences of some inexorable logic of collectivism or the interventionist state is that it can proceed without reference to any of the conditions which distinguish Britain from other Western societies. We should therefore expect the remaining capitalist democracies, which are all to some degree interventionist, to follow in its footsteps. In that respect, the argument from the 'logic' of the situation in an interventionist state suffers from much the same weakness as Goldthorpe's sociological account of Britain's inflation. Although Beer refers to the 'logic' of the situation, his account of Britain's problems has rather more to offer than any analysis conducted in such simplistic terms. The same cannot be said for the theorists of the 'new Hobbesian dilemma'.

VI

The 'strategy of equality' reconsidered

The notion that public expenditure on social-service provision had broadly egalitarian consequences was an important component of the consensus view of British social policy. For example, Marshall views the social services as providing the foundations of an equality of status with regard to the social aspects of citizenship, and in particular, as reducing the significance of differences in money incomes. Or again, Crosland presents the financing of public-service provision out of the increment of economic growth as a crucial means of promoting greater equality. This conception of the link between public expenditure on social services and equality could be understood in either a descriptive or a normative sense; that is, as a description of the state of affairs in post-war Britain or as indicating how a more equal society could be achieved. In this latter sense, the promotion of equality through public service provision is an important feature of what Tawney called the 'strategy of equality' (Tawney 1931), and we have seen that it plays a central role in Crosland's revisionist interpretation of socialist politics.

In fact, the evidence suggests that in Britain and elsewhere public expenditure on social-service provision has generally had markedly inegalitarian consequences. The second set of issues to be considered in this part of the book concerns the implications of this evidence for the 'strategy of equality'. The evidence itself is generally unambiguous, and it shows that in many areas of public-service provision, far from reducing the extent of differences of income and wealth, the overall effect of public expenditure is to exacerbate them (Field 1981; Halsey, Heath, and Ridge 1980; le Grand 1982; Townsend 1979). The problems come with trying to explain the lack of egalitarian impact. One approach is to suggest that the privileged will look after themselves. For example, Hirsch suggests that attempts to equalize the distribution of positional goods provokes resistance on the part of the privileged and the invention of new devices to preserve their privileged position. At a slightly more general level, Goldthorpe and Townsend offer structural explanations in terms of the resistance of the class structure, as a system of inequality, to egalitarian changes. Le Grand refers us to the 'ideology of inequality' and the self-interest of the wealthy. Other authors, for example Titmuss and George and Wilding (1976), see the problem as a matter of a conflict of social values.

This chapter considers the social and political conclusions that have been drawn from the evidence regarding the impact of public expenditure on social services. In the first instance we concentrate on Julian le Grand's argument in his influential book, *The Strategy of Equality*. This is a useful starting point for our discussion for two reasons. First, it brings together materials relating to different fields of social-service provision. It provides a valuable survey of the evidence and of the kinds of study that are available in the different fields. Secondly, and more important for our purposes, it is useful because of the clear political implications that it draws from its survey of the evidence. Its conclusion is that the 'strategy of equality' has clearly failed, and that therefore a far more radical attack on privilege is required. In the context of British politics this amounts to a kind of ultra-left conclusion to the effect that no amount of pussy-footing around with the system along the lines of Croslandite revisionism will get us very far. Similar conclusions are suggested by Townsend's study of poverty, Halsey's study of education, and in a rather different sense by Goldthorpe's study of social mobility in post-war Britain. We shall have to consider how far such conclusions may be justified by the arguments presented. This will involve, in particular, discussion of the uses of social principles, such as equality, in the assessment of policies and social conditions. It is easy enough for principles to be used as a means of condemning social conditions. Their use for more constructive purposes is not so straightforward.

THE FAILURE OF REFORMISM?

The argument of *The Strategy of Equality* is in three parts. The first part outlines the strategy of increasing social and economic equality by means of public expenditure on social services, on health, education, housing, and transport. Immediately after the short Introduction is a chapter called 'The Dreamers'. This suggests that Tawney, Crosland, and many others have been committed to the 'strategy of equality', and furthermore that it has been influential in bringing about the growth of public expenditure in Britain and other Western societies.

If we are to evaluate that 'strategy', le Grand argues, two things are necessary. First, we should clarify what we understand by 'equality'. For example, in respect of education, do we mean equality of opportunity (with no category of children being disadvantaged relative to others), equality of outcome (with all categories performing equally), equality of expenditure (so that resources are allocated equally to all categories), or something else? Le Grand has no difficulty in showing that these different kinds of equality are by no means equivalent. Equality of outcome is unlikely to be produced merely by providing equivalent educational opportunities to children from very different social backgrounds. Secondly, we should examine the evidence to see how far expenditure on the social services meets the objectives of the strategy with regard to the most important senses of equality. The greater part of le Grand's text is devoted to this second task. It shows that, in general, public expenditure on the provision of social services benefits the better off. It has not achieved equality, nor in most cases has it reduced inequality in any significant respect.

The final step in the argument is to conclude that the 'strategy of equality' has failed, and further, that while piecemeal reforms in the pattern of social services might improve things from an egalitarian standpoint, they would still leave the fundamental structure of inequality untouched. In le Grand's account a crucial aspect of that fundamental structure is the 'ideology of inequality' which, together with the self-interest of the wealthy, is the major obstacle to the realization of equality. The conclusion is that the 'strategy of equality' has failed primarily because it did not tackle that ideology directly. Instead of attacking inequalities at source – for example, by equalizing incomes – it tried to rely on redistribution after the event while leaving the underlying structure of inequality untouched.

Two important features of this argument are worth noting before we proceed to le Grand's survey of the evidence. First, it is only the second part that is reasonably well developed. The discussion of the distributional impact of public spending on education, health, housing, and transport is useful both as a presentation of the available evidence and of some of the technical and methodological issues at stake in its interpretation. The problem is that the rest of the argument is relatively weak. This means that there is at best a tenuous connection between le Grand's general political conclusions and his survey of the evidence on the distributional impact of spending on the social services.

In this respect, unfortunately, le Grand is in very good academic company. Townsend's 1979 study *Poverty in the United Kingdom* massively documents the facts of poverty (as he defines it) and inequality in Britain but devotes little space either to the transformation of social relations that would be required to eliminate poverty or to the social and political obstacles to its achievement. Here, too, the radical political conclusion to the book is not supported by the bulk of the evidence it provides. The Oxford Mobility studies of Halsey, Heath, and Ridge on education (1980), and Goldthorpe, on social mobility (1980), exhibit similar problems (Hindess 1981). Here is an extract from the conclusion to Goldthorpe's *Social Mobility and Class Structure in Modern Britain* (1980) which le Grand quotes in support of his concluding argument:

'The implication of the findings . . . therefore count as rather grave ones for the general strategy of egalitarian reform that has been widely adhered to among liberals and social democrats in modern Britain: briefly, the strategy of seeking to attack social inequalities via legislative and administrative measures of a piecemeal kind that can be carried through without venturing too far beyond the limits of 'consensus' politics. What our results would suggest – and the same point could be made by reference to research on various other topics – is that this strategy grossly misjudges the resistance that the class structure can offer to attempts to change it: or, to speak less figuratively, the flexibility and effectiveness with which the more powerful and advantaged groupings in society can use the resources at their disposal to preserve their privileged positions. There is, in other words, a serious underestimation of the forces maintaining the situation in which change is sought, relative to the force of the measures through which, it is supposed, change can be implemented.'

(Goldthorpe 1980: 252; quoted in le Grand 1982: 125)

Here, again, the problem is with the gap between the political concerns that apparently motivate the study, on the one hand, and the empirical materials and procedures in terms of which it is conducted, on the other. Goldthorpe tells us a great deal about the occupational mobility of men in England and Wales, and he disposes of several misconceptions. But, in spite of the radical conclusion quoted above, the question of the forces ranged against egalitarian politics receives only the most casual treatment.

In effect, these studies present impressive piles of data, but little by way of argument or evidence in direct support of the political conclusions which they seek to draw from their work. Whatever the technical quality of the evidence they do present, we should be extremely wary of the way political conclusions appear to be drawn from them. Returning to le Grand's study in particular, the 'strategy of equality' functions in his argument both as:

(1) A means of assessing social services; that is, as defining a set of social objectives against which current forms of provision can be measured.
(2) A strategy that was pursued and that provides a partial explanation of the present structure and organization of the social services.

Both aspects are important to le Grand's argument, and both, as we shall see, are problematic.

The other point to notice is that *The Strategy of Equality* falls into a well-established tradition of writing about the social services in Britain. This consists in assessing the overall social impact of the welfare state, or of changes in it, primarily in distributional terms. In effect, from the appearance of Titmuss's 'The Social Division of Welfare' (discussed in Chapter III above) there has been a wealth of studies showing that public expenditure on the social services is often markedly inegalitarian in its impact. Although le Grand makes use of these studies, he provides little systematic discussion of that tradition. The important point here is that the politics which he subsumes under the label of 'The Dreamers' (the title of his second chapter) is much less starry-eyed about public expenditure and its impact than he represents it. Indeed, much of the published work written from that perspective over the last thirty years or so has castigated the British welfare state precisely for its egalitarian failures, while remaining committed in broad terms to a tougher version of the 'strategy of equality'. That situation has begun to change in the last few years with the collapse of the old 'consensus' and the impact of Marxism in social-policy analysis. It is certainly true, as we have seen, that Marshall's 1950 essay presents what must now seem a rather naive assessment of the impact of the social services. But in general, le Grand scores easy points against 'Dreamers' (such as Crosland and Tawney) by oversimplifying the egalitarian politics they represent. We will return to this point.

INEQUALITY AND THE SOCIAL SERVICES

The central substantive chapters of *The Strategy of Equality* examine the impact of public expenditure on health care, education, housing, and transport. Le Grand does not directly examine the impact of spending on the personal social services or the provision of cash benefits. A preliminary point to notice in examining the distributional impact of the social services is that they do not themselves monitor the effects of their activities on inequality. The health services do not normally require information about the class background, wealth, or income of patients before deciding how or whether to treat them. Transport subsidies, with some exceptions, go to the providers of the services, rather than directly to users. Thus, although social-services agencies frequently provide statistical information about their services, it is not generally available in a form that is useful from the point of view of assessing their distributional impact.

This point is significant for two reasons. First, it suggests that the 'strategy of equality' has not occupied quite the central place in the organization of the social services that le Grand's political argument implies. If the social services were indeed established primarily to reduce inequality, it is somewhat surprising that they do so little to monitor their effectiveness in this respect.

Secondly, it follows that studies of that impact have to bring together and interpret evidence from a variety of different sources. Thus, much of le Grand's discussion is devoted to the technical assessment of the quality of the available evidence and the problems of its interpretation. These technical issues will not be considered here, but it is perhaps worth noting a general point about 'facts' in the social sciences. The 'facts' of the distributional impact of social-service expenditure are themselves complex constructs based on the interpretation of evidence that is limited and often collected for quite other purposes. These facts are generally open to dispute and to the possibility of alternative interpretation. This is not to say that what the 'facts' are is a matter of arbitrary choice. But they are always the outcome of specific techniques of construction and interpretation. Changes in the techniques of construction can sometimes produce strikingly different results. For example, changes introduced in 1982 in the presentation of unemployment statistics in Britain resulted in significantly lower totals.

If we take the case of public expenditure on health care, the DHSS do not provide data on expenditure on different income groups or classes. However, the General Household Survey conducted by the Office of Population Censuses and Surveys does provide data from a continuous survey of 32,000 people, and it questions respondents, among other things, about their state of health and use of the NHS. It is therefore possible, but difficult and time-consuming, to work out estimates of the uses of the NHS and costs of resources devoted to the treatment of different socio-economic groups. Le Grand classifies the population into the following categories: professionals, employers, and managers; intermediate and junior non-manual; skilled manual; semi- and unskilled manual. Using these categories he constructs two sets of figures for the distribution of NHS expenditure. One relates to the number of persons in each socio-economic group and the other relates to the number of persons in each socio-economic group reporting illness. His results show no consistent pattern of expenditure per person favouring either the 'higher' or the 'lower' socio-economic categories. But a very clear pattern of inequality emerges for expenditure per person reporting illness, with the 'higher' socio-economic categories receiving considerably more than the 'lower', with the 'highest' group (professional, etc.) receiving over 40 per cent more than the lowest (le Grand 1982: 25–6).

These results should be interpreted with caution. Their calculation involves a number of estimates and guesses, and le Grand suggests a number of respects in which they might be disputed. Nevertheless, the general impression of a systematic pattern of inequality can be further supported in two ways. First, le Grand cites a number of studies which suggest that GPs spend more time with patients from the higher socio-economic categories. So the cost per consultation will tend to be greater for patients in the higher categories. The same is probably true for out-patient consultations and other hospital treatment. This implies that the above figures probably under-estimate the inequality of NHS provision. Secondly, it might be suggested that the differences in expenditure per person reporting illness arise because members of the higher categories have different diseases, which, as it happens, are also more expensive to treat. In fact there is little evidence to support this view. The General Household Survey itself indicates that the distribution of disease is relatively uniform across socio-economic categories, and that the lower categories have a higher incidence of almost all forms of disease. The differences in expenditure per ill person do not reflect different illnesses. We must therefore conclude that members of the lower socio-economic categories on average make significantly less use of, or are given significantly less assistance by, the NHS.

How should these differences be explained? Le Grand cites a number of studies which suggest that there are substantial differences in the use of the NHS by members of the different categories, that people in the lower categories make less use of the facilities of the health service. These differences in use are a function first of decisions by patients themselves and, secondly, of decisions by medical personnel. Individuals decide whether or not to contact the health service, but many of the subsequent decisions about their treatment are out of their hands. For both sets of decisions there are reasons to expect them to favour greater use of the health services by the middle classes.

Consider, first, decisions by the patients themselves. Here le Grand offers a 'rational choice' model of behaviour in which individuals decide on a visit to the doctor (or whatever) on the basis of the perceived costs and benefits. The benefits will be those of any expected improvement in health. The costs will be primarily those of time and money. Le Grand argues that the costs of using a 'free' service are likely to be higher for people from the lower socio-economic categories. Time spent travelling will be higher because they are more dependent on public transport and the areas in which they live are poorly endowed with medical facilities. Waiting time will often be higher because working-class households are much less likely to have access to telephones and will therefore find it more difficult to make appointments. As for the monetary costs, members of the higher socio-economic categories are unlikely to lose pay for time spent visiting the doctor during working hours. Those in manual occupations may lose pay for any time they take off. As for the decisions by medical personnel, there is considerable evidence to show that working-class patients are treated differently from members of other classes. For example, middle- and upper-class patients are more frequently referred by their GPs to hospital than are working-class patients: 'Costs greater, benefits lower: it is not surprising that the lower social groups demand less medical care than the higher ones, even when there is no charge' (le Grand 1982: 34).

In fact, there are serious problems with 'rational choice' models of behaviour (Hindess 1984). Le Grand's account presents us with individuals responding to a given pattern of costs and benefits. It does little to tell us why the costs and benefits are as they are; why, for example, GPs and other medical personnel tend to devote more time and attention to their middle-class patients. That is regrettable, but it is clearly not an inherent feature of public expenditure on health service provision. For the rest notice two points. The first is that a service which is free at the point of use (such as medical consultations on the NHS) is not necessarily without cost to the user. Secondly, the behaviour of medical personnel can significantly affect the pattern of use of health service facilities. That point has clear implications for equality, but we shall see that there are wider issues at stake here.

Turning to the effects of health service expenditure on the distribution of health, le Grand shows that class inequalities have not changed significantly since the introduction of the NHS. This result should not be too surprising since death rates and ill health among the population at large are not much affected by the availability of health care. This is not to say that medical treatment makes no difference to those who receive it. Rather, it is that such differences as it does make do not much affect population aggregates. Overall, le Grand concludes that inequalities in the costs of health care, its use, and outcomes have not been significantly reduced by the NHS. Little can be done by the health service to remedy this state of affairs since the principal determinants of inequality are not within its control: they are themselves the result of the 'basic structure of social and economic inequality' (le Grand 1982: 51).

Turning now to education, housing, and transport, the character of the evidence is rather different in each of these areas, and it poses different problems of interpretation. Nevertheless, the general conclusions are very similar. Most public expenditure on education goes on primary and secondary schools, and it therefore has some equalizing effect. But a significant proportion also goes on post-compulsory education, to sixth-form education, further-education colleges, universities, and polytechnics. These are used disproportionately by children from the higher socio-economic groups. Here, too, le Grand makes use of a 'rational choice' model to account for some of the differences between classes. The result is that public expenditure on non-compulsory education has striking anti-egalitarian consequences. Le Grand suggests that there is a strong case for reducing state support here.

In each of the areas le Grand examines, the general conclusion is that the overall effect of public expenditure on these services favours the better-off. Far from reducing the significance of differences in money income, as Marshall had thought, public expenditure on these social services tends to multiply them.

Two further issues should be raised before we conclude this section. The first concerns the overall impact of the welfare state. We have noted that le Grand's discussion does not cover spending on personal social services or cash benefits. When these are taken into account the broad effects of *all* social spending are generally pro-poor (see Davies and Piachaud 1983). Furthermore, discussion of the impact of the welfare state should not be restricted to its redistributive effects. Le Grand suggests that there may be reasons other than a concern for equality for public expenditure on service provision. Social policy may have an impact on the maintenance of minimum standards and in ensuring that certain services are available to all members of the population. It may also have consequences for economic growth and aspects of the quality of life that are difficult to quantify (see George and Wilding 1984).

Secondly, two distinct modes of public spending are involved in housing provision. First there are direct expenditures on the provision of council housing, option mortgages, rent allowances, improvement grants, and so on. But there 'are also sizeable tax expenditures associated with housing, that is tax reliefs, primarily for owner occupiers, which reduce the government's tax revenue below the level that would obtain in their absence' (le Grand 1982: 82). The latter is an example of what Titmuss calls fiscal welfare. Le Grand includes it in his calculation of the net effect of public spending on housing and concludes that it strongly favours the better off. That argument raises the question of how far tax allowances can be considered a form of public spending. We raise the issue here because it goes against a conviction that is strongly held by many economic liberals. We shall see, for example, that Friedman treats income as belonging to the individual who receives it. In that case any tax would be an imposition on the individual concerned. That perspective clearly plays a part in many popular perceptions of taxation. If tax is an imposition, then tax allowances are hardly a form of spending on a par with direct expenditure on the provision of services.

We return to this issue in Chapter VIII. For the present, notice that there is a considerable difference between regarding tax as an imposition on the tax-payer, at best a regrettable necessity, and regarding tax allowances as a form of government expenditure.

THE DEVELOPMENT OF THE SOCIAL SERVICES

The general conclusion of the central substantive chapters of *The Strategy of Equality* is that public expenditure on the provision of social services in Britain has not reduced inequality, and further that in some areas it has tended to multiply the effects of differences in income and wealth. At that level the book does little more than bring together and summarize findings that have been available for some time, and, with some qualifications, that conclusion is entirely acceptable. Had things been left at that point, there would be little in *The Strategy of Equality* to dispute. However, le Grand attempts to use his conclusions regarding the distributional impact of social-service expenditure in support of a more general political argument. Unfortunately, while the substantive argument is reasonably well developed, the more general argument is not. We have noted that a similar discrepancy between empirical materials and the political conclusions that are drawn from them, can also be found in some of the work of Townsend, Halsey, Goldthorpe, and others.

These authors use relatively well-developed empirical investigations of the extent of poverty, educational inequality, and the like, to bolster what amounts to the merest gesture of an argument against reformism. Le Grand uses his empirical materials to mount a case against the 'strategy of equality' and in favour of what seems to be a more radical alternative. It is this more general political argument that is our main concern in the remainder of this chapter. We have noted that le Grand's argument uses the 'strategy of equality' in two ways. First, it is used to specify some desirable social objectives against which the current state of social-service provision can be measured. In that sense, the goal of the 'strategy of equality' has clearly not been realized in modern Britain. Secondly, the 'strategy' is used as a partial explanation of the current state of affairs. This second usage is important, because it is only if the strategy has been implemented that it is possible to talk of its failure. We begin with this usage of the 'strategy' as explanation, returning later to the awkward question of the use of 'equality' in assessing social conditions.

In effect, the argument is as follows. The strategy of equality has been implemented in Britain through the expansion of public spending on health, education, and other services. The evidence shows that the actual distribution of expenditure and its results are strongly anti-egalitarian in character. The conclusion for egalitarians is therefore that the 'strategy of equality' has proved unsuccessful, and it should be replaced by something stronger. The first step, then, is the claim that that 'strategy' 'has played a dominating role in the growth of public expenditure in Britain, and indeed throughout the world' (*ibid.*: 3). And again we are told that the pursuit of equality has been a 'major justification' (*ibid.*: 8) for the massive post-war expansion of government spending on the social services. Similar claims are made with regard to each of the service areas examined by le Grand. In health care 'a major justification for state intervention has been the attainment of some kind of equality' (*ibid.*: 24), while in education 'perhaps the major motivation has been the pursuit of equality' (*ibid.*: 54). In themselves these formulations would be sufficiently imprecise as to be unexceptionable were it not for the weight that le Grand subsequently puts on the claim that non-egalitarian conditions are evidence of the failure of the 'strategy of equality':

> 'public expenditure on the social services has not achieved equality in any of its interpretations. . . . Nor does there seem to be much prospect of retrieving the situation through any piecemeal reform. Basically, the forces which created the inequalities in the first place and which perpetuate them seem to be too strong to be resisted through indirect methods such as public expenditure on the social services. Rather, the strategy of equality has to be aimed at tackling those forces directly.'
>
> (*ibid.*: 137)

In the light of that conclusion it is unfortunate that le Grand did not subject 'those forces' to more serious investigation. For the rest, his argument exaggerates the significance of egalitarian considerations in the establishment of the social services. In particular, it provides no analysis of the place of those considerations in the organizational structures of the various services relative to other concerns and objectives. It is only because he fails to address these questions that le Grand can interpret evidence of the distributional impact of social-service spending as signs of the failure of the 'strategy of equality'. The following examples illustrate the significance of this point.

EQUALITY AND THE NHS

Consider first the organizational structure of health service provision. The following points are based on the excellent short discussion of the development of the NHS in Klein's *The Politics of the National Health Service* (1983). For present purposes the most important thing to notice is that egalitarian considerations played a very limited role in establishing the NHS and in determining its organizational structure. While there were certainly disputes about the detailed organization of the proposed new service, the general idea that there should be a *national* health service had widespread support across the political spectrum. Much of that support came from those who were in no sense egalitarians. The idea of a national service had considerable support within the medical profession, not primarily on egalitarian grounds, but rather for technocratic and administrative reasons. For example, there was concern about what were perceived as the inefficiencies and irrationalities of the mixture of private, charity, and local-government helath services that had developed in Britain. A properly *national* service was seen, in contrast, as a more rational and efficient form of provision. Or again, there was the desire of consultants to have access to the most advanced medical technologies in their fields, something that many locally financed services could not be expected to provide.

Of course, there were features of the NHS that were established at least in part for egalitarian reasons, notably the decision to have a centrally administered service. Morrison had argued against that decision and in favour of local government administration on broadly democratic grounds:

'It is possible to argue that almost every local government function, taken by itself, could be administered more efficiently in the technical sense under a national system, but if we wish local government to thrive – as a school of political and democratic education as well as a method of administration – we must consider the general effect on local government of each particular proposal. It would be disastrous if we allowed local government to languish by whittling away its most constructive and interesting functions.'

(Morrison 1945; quoted in Klein 1983: 18–19)

Proposals for local government control were resisted by the medical profession on professional grounds – they didn't want elected politicians interfering in health service administration. It was also opposed by Bevan in the Labour Party on the grounds of efficiency and equity: 'Under any local government system there will tend to be a better service in the richer areas, a worse service in the poorer' (Bevan, 1945; quoted by Klein 1983: 19). Egalitarian considerations certainly played a part in Bevan's case for a nationally administered service. The NHS that was finally launched in July 1948 was designed 'to universalise the best', 'to provide the people of Great Britain, no matter where they may be, with the same level of service' (Klein 1983: 25). In this respect, at least, the NHS has made some progress – admittedly very limited. The organizational and administrative obstacles to a significant redistribution of resources within a centrally administered system are not as easy to overcome as Bevan originally imagined. Nevertheless, Klein suggests that regional variations in Britain are 'less conspicuous than in most other developed countries: even in Russia, where there is a totally planned economy, large scale geographical variations persist' (*ibid.*: 150).

To conclude, although egalitarian considerations did play a part in the formation of the NHS, that part was always strictly limited. Neither the medical and administrative personnel of the NHS, nor the bulk of politicians and civil servants concerned with it, regarded the NHS primarily as a vehicle for bringing about equality of treatment between classes. In view of the importance of other concerns (political, medical, and organizational) in the establishing of the NHS, it should not be too surprising that equality between classes has not been achieved. In presenting equality as 'a major justification' for establishing the NHS, le Grand drastically oversimplifies the complexity of the state machine and the diversity of social interests, concerns, and objectives that contribute to its organization and functioning. The same problem arises in his treatment of other policy areas.

THE IMPACT OF POLITICS

If *The Strategy of Equality* overstates the role of egalitarian considerations in the establishment of the NHS and other social services, it also tends to overestimate the impact of political decisions on their functioning and organization. With a few notable exceptions, the decisions of democratically elected governments in peacetime operate at the margins of existing patterns of organization and expenditure. In effect, this means that governments maintain the bulk of the activities and organizations they inherit, and they attempt to shift the balance in one direction or another. Governments are rarely able to introduce entirely new patterns of organization or spending without considerable preparation beforehand. On the whole, changes are introduced in an incremental fashion, leaving the greater part of the state machine intact. We made a similar point about policy instruments in discussion of Crosland's arguments in Chapter II above.

Returning to the case of the NHS, there is certainly a sense in which its establishment in July 1948 must be regarded as a significant new development. Nevertheless, most of its plant and equipment, and the bulk of its medical and administrative personnel were inherited from its charity, private-authority and local-authority predecessors. New hospital building and other changes have altered the inherited structure, but after almost forty years important elements of the earlier geographical inequalities remain. The incremental character of those changes and the costs involved in them are clearly recognized in Klein's remark that

> 'there is nothing wrong with the policy instruments for promoting progress towards the achievement of geographical equity which could not be cured by a faster economic growth rate: by factors outside the control of the health care policy-makers.'
>
> (Klein 1983: 150)

To take a more recent example, consider the hostility of leading members of the Thatcher government towards the NHS. Their valiant efforts to dismantle the NHS have met with some limited success, but in general they have achieved little more than incremental damage to the service they inherited in 1979.

A second point to notice from our earlier discussion of policy instruments is that governments always have a variety of objectives with some bearing on social-service expenditure. The obvious example here concerns the place of public spending in overall economic management. In his discussion of the fate of the 1942 Beveridge Report in *Inequality in Britain* (1981) Field notes how its proposals were watered down partly on grounds of their likely cost, first as a result of Treasury pressure before preparation of the final draft, and later by the Labour cabinet. Le Grand himself notes that in 1978/79 'expenditure on the social services comprised nearly 40 per cent of all government expenditure in Great Britain, and well over half of the expenditure on goods and services' (le Grand 1982: 7). British economic management over at least the last thirty years or so has not been conspicuously successful. It would be astonishing if the pattern of social-service provision had not been affected by erratic budgetary decisions deriving from economic-policy considerations. Indeed, given the incremental character of changes in these services, short-term cuts (affecting, say, planned capital spending) can have drastic long-term consequences. But the important point here is simply that government decisions affecting the NHS or other services rarely point in a single, well-defined policy direction.

Finally, it is worth remembering that governments come and go, and they often have very different objectives. In the case of Labour governments, which might be expected to be most susceptible to egalitarian concerns, there is considerable evidence (in the Castle and Crossman diaries and in Crosland's biography) that they frequently lacked any clear sense of priorities. Even if we were to suppose that they were strongly committed to egalitarian objectives, which is itself implausible, it would be a mistake to suppose that they had a clear idea of what might be done to achieve them. The post-war period has also seen many years of Conservative governments, not at all committed to equality.

We have argued that the pattern of public expenditure on the provision of social services is the result of incremental changes to a pre-existing pattern of expenditure. Many, but not all, of these changes were introduced by governments and ministers of various political persuasions. In some cases egalitarian considerations have played a part, but in others they have not. Overall, the pattern of public spending has not been dominated by the objective of achieving a significantly more equal society. It is worth noting that there has been a considerable expansion of public expenditure on social services in all the advanced capitalist economies since the war – and that in some of these countries egalitarianism has been considerably less influential than it has in Britain (Wilensky 1975). This is not to say that egalitarian concerns have had no impact on the development of the post-war British welfare state. But they have certainly not had the importance that le Grand's argument requires. In so far as equality has been a consideration, it has always had to co-exist with other considerations and other policy concerns and objectives. If that has proved to be a problem for the 'strategy of equality', it would also be a problem for whatever policy instruments might conceivably be employed by governments to promote equality.

PRINCIPLES AND SOCIAL CONDITIONS

There are two further issues to note before concluding this part of our discussion. We have seen that the pattern of expenditure on social-service provision in Britain cannot be regarded simply as the outcome of a failed attempt to achieve equality. Egalitarian considerations have played a part in the development of social policy, but they have done so in conjunction with a variety of competing interests, concerns and objectives. We should therefore expect some discrepancy between the pattern of social-policy provision and the requirements of egalitarian principles. What we have to consider then are the implications of such discrepancies for the political assessment of social conditions and of actual or proposed policies. There are two related issues here. One concerns the significance attached to equality rather than to other considerations. The second and more general issue concerns the place of general principles, such as equality or liberty, in the assessment of social conditions and the evaluation of proposals for change. We return to that issue in Chapter 9.

In concentrating on the distributional impact of expenditure on social-service provision there is a danger of neglecting other aspects of the functioning of these services. Le Grand argues, quite correctly, that there may be good reasons for public expenditure on the provision of goods and services even if its result is not to promote greater equality. In some cases, for example, a publicly provided service or a subsidy to private supplier may be the only ways to ensure that a service is available at all for many people. But a more general issue is at stake here which concerns the discussion of public expenditure largely in terms of outcomes conceived in terms of the provision of greater or lesser quantities of welfare.

Consider the example of public spending on the provision of housing. Le Grand examines the overall distributional effects of direct and indirect expenditure on housing and concludes that they operate in favour of the better off. From an egalitarian perspective this is clearly an undesirable state of affairs. But to leave the analysis at this point is to ignore other significant differences between expenditures on tax relief and, say, on subsidizing local authority housing. A recent discussion of the quality of public housing provision included the following passage:

> 'More than 300,000 units, mostly in comparatively new buildings, have been officially classified as "difficult to let", a euphemism for not fit to live in. Strangely, this waste of millions, possibly billions of pounds, perpetrated by councils of all political persuasions, has raised no public outcry, is not regarded as a national scandal, but rather as a well-intentioned, excusable mistake.'
>
> (*Guardian*, 31 January 1983)

This raises the important question for the present discussion of how far expenditure on the provision of housing results in unequivocal benefits for the recipients of that service. The quantitative aspects of public spending on housing are certainly important, but they should not blind us to questions of the organization and functioning of public-housing administration and how it impinges on actual or potential tenants. In *Inequality in Britain* Field argues for a system of cash benefits partly on the grounds that the element of paternalistic control inherent in public-housing management is an infringement on freedom. Stretton has argued that socialists should favour private home ownership on similar grounds (Stretton 1983). It is not necessary to agree with these arguments to see that there is more to public spending on housing than the question of its distributional effects. Similar points could obviously be made with regard to public spending on health and education. The danger of assessing social-service provision primarily in quantitative terms is that it tends to suggest that what is provided is indeed greater or lesser quantities of welfare. We should not accept that suggestion too readily.

Far from showing that the 'strategy of equality' has been tried and failed, the record shows that it has played at most a limited role in the development of the British social services. Social-service expenditure has not produced a significantly more equal society in Britain. But to say that is merely to say that egalitarian politics have not been the dominant element in British politics over the last forty or so years, and they have certainly not had things all their own way. That may be unfortunate, but it is hardly a surprise, and it is certainly not a new discovery.

VII

Marxism

The collapse of the old consensus has seen the growth of alternative approaches to the analysis of social policy. Marxism and liberalism each bring a distinctive political perspective to bear on their analysis of British society and the place of social policy within it, but for all the differences between them, we shall see that they share a common essentialization of the market. Marxism analyses politics and the state primarily in terms of the struggle between contending classes. This means that social policy in a capitalist society can be seen both as serving the interests of the capitalist ruling class and as the product of class struggle. A *Marxism Today* article published in the first year of the Thatcher administration presents the issue as follows:

'On the one hand it is important to give full weight to the basic economic imperatives of the capitalist mode of production: the devising of new means of exploiting labour, the need for the continuous accumulation of capital and the necessity for maintaining profitability. If you look at the Welfare State from this standpoint, then you will see its origins as lying fundamentally in the needs of capitalist exploitation. . . .

'On the other hand, it is important to avoid the rigid economic determinism which is the danger of a perspective on the Welfare State which lays too great an emphasis on the needs of capitalism. The role of class struggle is also crucial to our understanding of the development of the Welfare State. In Britain, the Labour Party and the trade union movement have been vital to the growth of education, health and social services.'

(Leonard 1979: 8)

The welfare state is therefore both an instrument in the hands of the capitalist ruling class and a little island of socialism created by the working class in the sea of capitalist society. Marxists have devoted considerable ingenuity to resolving the tensions between these two positions, and they have done so in a large number of different ways. Rather than attempt to survey the variety of Marxist analyses of social policy, this chapter concentrates on one book, Ian Gough's *The Political Economy of the Welfare State* (1979), while referring to other Marxist positions from time to time. Gough's book provides a clearly-written and comprehensive account of the British welfare state, and it is a sophisticated example of its kind. However, we begin with a short discussion of Marxism's account of classes and the structure of society, before moving on to consider what it has to say about the state and its welfare policies.

CLASSES AND THE STRUCTURE OF SOCIETY

As a theory of social structure and social change, Marxism brings together two fundamental themes. The first is stated in a famous passage of *The Communist Manifesto* :

'The history of all hitherto existing society is the history of class struggles. Freeman and slave, patrician and plebeian, lord and serf, guild-master and journeyman, in a word, oppressor and oppressed, stood in constant opposition to one another, carried on an uninterrupted, now hidden, now open fight, a fight that each time ended, either in a revolutionary reconstitution of society at large, or in the common ruin of the contending classes.'

(Marx and Engels [1848] 1976: 482)

There are two elements here. First, fundamental social changes come about as the outcome of struggles between social forces, and secondly, the basic social forces engaged in these struggles are classes. Both have been disputed by non-Marxists, and it is clearly possible to accept the first without accepting the second.

The second fundamental theme concerns the relationships between the different parts of a society. A schematic outline is given in Marx's preface to *A Contribution to the Critique of Political Economy*. First, there is an economic foundation involving relations of production and material forces of production:

'on which arises [secondly] a legal and political superstructure and
to which correspond [thirdly] definite forms of social consciousness.
The mode of production of material life conditions the general
process of social, political and intellectual life.'

(Marx [1859] 1971: 21)

Marx presents the contradiction between forces and relations of
production as the general mechanism of social development, and he
goes on to insist that changes in the economic foundation 'lead
sooner or later to the transformation of the whole immense superstructure' (*ibid*.: 21). He also distinguishes the real content of struggles
from the conscious forms in which they are fought out. This is
not the place for an extended commentary on Marx's enigmatic
formulations (but see Cutler *et al*. 1977, Parts II and III). However,
it is worth noting that there is room for considerable dispute as to
the precise interpretation of the relations referred to as 'on which
arises' and 'to which corresponds'. Again, the qualification 'sooner
or later' suggests that there is room for considerable discrepancies
between the economic foundation and the superstructure that is
supposed to arise on or correspond to it.

How do these themes fit together? On the one hand, the motor of
history is class struggle, and on the other hand, it is the internal
dynamic of the economic foundation. The answer is that classes are
fundamentally constituted within the economic foundation by relations
of production. In other words, the character of the economy (1)
generates the classes that fight it out in a society and (2) determines
the basic character of politics and law (and therefore the state) and
'forms of social consciousness'. Thus the dominant forms of politics
and ideology are supposed both to reflect the character of the economic
base and to serve the interests of the ruling class.

In the case of capitalist society, the relations of production specify
two fundamental classes: a class of capitalists (bourgeoisie) who own
the means of production, and a class of workers (proletariat) who do
not. Capitalists start with capital, and they buy in everything they
need for production to take place (raw materials, machinery, buildings,
and the labour power of workers). The workers start with nothing
but their labour power, which they sell by the hour (or day or week)
to capitalists in return for wages. Workers use their wages to buy

from capitalists, and what they buy are subsistence goods which allow them to reproduce their labour power ready to sell it again for yet more wages. Capitalists sell their products to other capitalists or to workers. Then the whole process starts over again, with the workers more or less where they started and the capitalists where they started *plus* profit.

One of the great achievements generally claimed for Marx is his explanation of the source of capitalist profit. What makes profit possible, according to Marx, is the fact that the working class as a whole produces more than it consumes. That, of course, is true of the exploited class in any mode of production. What distinguishes the position of the capitalist working class from the position of serfs or slaves is that their labour power and other elements of the production process take the form of commodities; that is, as items with a definite money value. Interactions between capitalists and workers have the appearance of equal exchange: capitalists buy labour power from workers at its market value, and they sell workers consumption goods at their value. The value form of these exchanges therefore represents the exploitation of one class by another as if it were a process of equal exchange.

This account is, of course, the merest sketch of a more complex analysis, but it is sufficient to indicate two fundamental sources of conflict in the relations between capitalists and the working class. First, in the process of production there are conflicts arising out of capitalists' more or less successful attempts to control the activities of their workforces. Secondly, there are conflicting interests arising out of the different market positions of capitalists and workers, as buyers and sellers, respectively, of labour power. The differential positions of capitalists and workers define conflicting objective interests that are supposed to be inherent in capitalist relations of production. The struggles which they generate will continue until the organized working class succeeds in overthrowing capitalism and we move towards a society in which there are no contending classes, in which, as the bitter Russian joke has it, the exploitation of man by man is replaced by its opposite.

The underlying optimism of Marx's analysis need not concern us here, but several other issues should be noted. First, the market plays a fundamental role in Marx's account of the process of capitalist exploitation. More precisely, exploitation depends on a combination of market relations between enterprises and of market relations between capitalists and workers. Given that account of exploitation, it is tempting to construct an opposition between socialism and the market which parallels in some respects the oppositions (between citizenship or social policy and the market) which we found in the works of Marshall and Titmuss. In these terms a move away from market relations (e.g. free medical services, subsidized housing and transport, government control of basic industries, etc.) would appear as at least the beginnings of socialism. It is in that sense that nationalization and the welfare state, for all their limitations, can be seen as islands of socialism in a capitalist sea. Conversely, any expansion of market relations can be seen as an anti-socialist measure. On that point Marxists and their liberal opponents are agreed. We return to this essentialization of 'the market' in the following chapter.

Secondly, capitalist societies contain many people who do not fit neatly into either of the positions of capitalist and worker distinguished above. Amongst capitalist employees, for example, there are highly paid specialists and managers who would be difficult to locate as members of the working class. Or, again, it is debatable whether bank or building-society employees could be regarded as producers of value, and therefore as exploited in Marx's sense. There are various kinds of state employees who produce no marketed goods or services. Finally, there are substantial minorities who are neither engaged in nor seeking paid employment. The problem is not that Marxist class analysis cannot find class positions for these groups, but rather that there are considerable disputes about where precisely they should be located.

Definitions of the working class may be relatively broad or relatively narrow. In his discussion of the main contemporary forms of Marxist class analysis, for example, Wright shows that they give estimates ranging from 20 per cent to 88 per cent of the proportion of the working class in the American population (Wright 1980). Again, some Marxists insist that there all politically significant strata and categories of the population belong to classes (Poulantzas 1976) while others invoke politically significant categories (Hobsbawm 1984, 1985 for example, refers to women, youth, etc.) that clearly cut across class lines however these are identified. Finally, there are

Marxists who argue that classes are constituted in the course of class struggle, so that what the boundaries are between one class and another is not determined simply by the relations of production in the economy (Przeworski, 1985). If history is the history of class struggles, then these differences as to the identification of classes can have important implications for political analysis. Much of the debate around Hobsbawm's analysis of the prospects for the Labour Party has turned on this question of class politics (Hobsbawm 1985; Jacques and Mulhern 1980; Fine *et al.* 1984).

But finding the correct location of various sections of the population is by no means the only problem facing Marxist class analysis. There are also serious problems concerning the connections that are supposed to hold between classes (however identified), on the one hand, and the organizations, ideologies, and issues of political life, on the other. It is difficult to deny that major social changes often involve struggles between contending social forces. It is less clear that those struggles are necessarily the motor of history – we have seen that Marxism itself is in two minds on this point – or that they are primarily structured around class differences. In contemporary Britain, for example, there are numerous organizations and groups engaged in political activities of the most diverse kinds – political parties, trades unions, capitalist enterprises, churches, state agencies, various women's and feminist groups, pro- and anti-abortion campaigns, environmental pressure groups, and so on – but there is no sense in which the bourgeoisie and the working class as such directly confront each other. Some of these groups and organizations claim to represent class interests, many others do not – although there may well be activists within them who do see politics in class terms. But it is one thing to say that the language of class provides some political groups and activists with terms of political analysis, and quite another to agree that politics *is* class struggle. We return below to this question of the relationship between classes and politics in Marxist analysis.

CAPITALISM AND THE STATE

Finally, it is important to recognize the systemic character of capitalism in Marxist analyses. What is at stake here is the idea of a structured social whole or totality characterized by definite structural properties or laws of motion. The explanation for developments within capitalist society are not ultimately to be found in the decisions of individuals. On the contrary, their decisions and actions are themselves the products of structural exigencies given by their location within the system as a whole. For example, it is often argued that capitalist enterprises are constrained to seek to maximize profits, irrespective of the motives of their owners or managers. The supposed systemic character of capitalism appears in two important respects in Marxist discussion. First, capitalism is said to be characterized by definite tendencies or laws of motion. Gough presents the main dynamic tendencies of capitalism in the following terms:

'The development of the productive forces, concentration of capital, dissolution of previous modes of production, and the establishment of a world economic system: these are all the results of the impetus of capital accumulation. The crucial point to note is that all are the unplanned result of a system which has its own autonomy and dynamic. Individual persons, whether capitalists or workers, are pressed by the "dull compulsion of economic forces" to undertake actions which result in the tendencies noted above. Nobody can escape them whilst the system (and it is a world system) lasts.'

(Gough 1979: 29)

My co-authors and I have discussed the problems of relying on historical tendencies for the purposes of political analysis (Cutler *et al*. 1978: Conclusion), and some of these problems are now widely recognized on the left.

Secondly, there is a marked tendency towards functional explanation. In Marx's schematic outline of the component parts of a society and the relations between them in the Preface to *A Contribution to the Critique of Political Economy* [1859] it seems that the political and legal superstructure and the 'forms of social consciousness' are determined (in ways that remain to be specified) by the economic foundation of society. They serve to keep capitalist relations of production in existence: the state keeps the working class under control and stops it taking over the means of production; the dominant ideology legitimizes the system; the family and education reproduce the capitalist labour force; the welfare state reproduces non-working sections of the population and it plays a part in reproducing the labour force, and so on. In effect, the whole system works so as to reproduce the existing pattern of relations between classes.

It is worth insisting on the functional character of much Marxist analysis since Marxism is often presented as anti-functionalist and many Marxists regard functionalism as inherently conservative. Gough claims that functionalism ignores 'the fact that history is also a succession of qualitatively distinct modes of production, and hence ignores the role of classes, class conflict and revolutionary rupture in human history' (Gough 1979: 9). Functionalism is the analysis of the parts of some larger system in terms of the functions they are held to perform for the system as a whole – so that reference to the function is seen as providing at least a partial explanation. Probably the best-known examples of functionalism in sociology are the structural-functionalist positions which dominated American sociology, and sociology textbooks, for most of the post-war period. Sociological functionalism analysed societies as systems organized around common values and as facing particular problems as systems (e.g. problems of internal equilibrium and problems of boundary relations with the physical environment and other systems). Different parts of society could then be analysed in terms of their contributions to the maintenance of value consensus and the resolution of those systemic problems.

Now, Marxism is clearly not a functionalism of that kind. It denies that there can be value consensus in a class-divided society, and it insists on the role of class struggle. But it also insists that the state is the state of the ruling class, that the ruling ideas are the ideas of the ruling class, and so on. Much of the explanation offered in Marxist discussions of the state or ideology is in terms of their function in the maintenance or reproduction of the existing system of class exploitation. Some examples will be given below.

Nevertheless, it would be wrong to suggest that Marxists are unaware of the problems of functional analysis. Where some insist that significant features of the state are to be analysed in terms of the needs of capitalism, others insist on the role of class struggle (see Holloway and Picciotto 1978, for examples of both). Sometimes functional analysis is combined with an insistence on class struggle and societal contradictions. For example, some of Offe's analyses of the modern welfare state treat it in terms of both the interdependence of sub-systems (in which the welfare state is interpreted as operating so as to reproduce the economy and structures of socialization) and the contradictory relations between them (Offe 1984, especially the first essay). As an example of the latter, consider the contradictions between decommodification and commodification. Decommodification refers to the welfare state's intervention in the market economy to ensure that the pattern of distribution is modified by politically defined 'welfare' considerations; for example, in relation to the provision of education, health care, subsidized housing, and so on. In the absence of such interventions, Offe suggests, the unregulated market would generate explosive political conditions. The welfare state therefore subverts the market in order to sustain the conditions of its continued functioning. The growth of what Marshall terms 'citizenship' is necessary for the functioning of the capitalist market economy, and its effect is to undermine the rigours of the market. In effect, the welfare state is here analysed in terms of its contradictory attempts to perform an impossible function.

For a different example of Marxism's ambiguous relationship with functional analysis, consider Gough's discussion in *The Political Economy of the Welfare State*. In the section immediately following his account of the laws of motion of capitalism Gough insists that

> '[t]he autonomous dynamic of capitalism provides the starting point for a materialist analysis of the welfare state. The course of capital accumulation continually generates new 'needs' or 'requirements' in the arena of social policy'
>
> (Gough 1979: 32)

And again, Gough follows Miliband's account (1969) of why the state serves the interests of the capitalist class. Miliband gives three explanations, the most important of which, in Gough's view,

> 'is in terms of the "structural constraints" which its insertion within the capitalist mode of production imposes on the state. Whatever the class background of state personnel, or the pressures exerted on the state from outside, the capitalist economy "has its

own rationality to which any government or state must sooner or later submit, and usually sooner".'

(Gough 1979: 42)

Notice how this position flatly contradicts Crosland's confident assertion that 'the government can exert any influence it likes on income distribution, and can also determine within broad limits the division of total output' (Crosland 1956: 27). Government cannot exert 'any influence it likes', because sooner or later even a socialist government will be compelled to give way to the rationality of the capitalist economy. It is partly for this reason that Miliband argued, in *Parliamentary Socialism* (1973), that a party committed to the advance of socialism primarily by parliamentary means was bound to fail.

A few pages later Gough insists on the inadequacy of functional explanation, warning against the assumption

'that the state responds to the functional requirements of capital. This is quite unjustified. The fact that some function is required for the accumulation or reproduction of capital (like the reproduction of labour power) tells us nothing about whether or not the state meets those requirements or the manner in which it responds to them.'

(Gough 1979: 50–1)

The difficulty with Gough's position is clear. If the requirements of capital accumulation are not satisfied, the accumulation cannot take place. If the dynamic of accumulation is indeed 'autonomous', then the state has no option but to meet those requirements; if political struggle may produce a situation in which the state does not meet those requirements, then there can be no autonomous dynamic. Here and throughout his book Gough offers a functional analysis with one hand and takes it away with the other. In fact, this is a recurrent feature of Marxist analysis: it is functionalist and antifunctionalist, but not consistently either.

What then can we say about Marxist analyses of the state and its welfare and social-policy activities? On the one hand, social policy is to be analysed in terms of the performance of various functions for the maintenance or reproduction of capitalism, and on the other, it is to be analysed in terms of the effects of class struggle. Different Marxist analyses produce different uneasy and more or less complex combinations of these approaches. Beginning with the state, Marxism starts off from the basic position that, as Lenin puts it in *The State and Revolution*, it 'is an organ of class rule, an organ for the oppression of one class by another; it is the creation of "order", which legalises and perpetuates this oppression by moderating the conflict between classes' (Lenin [1917] 1964: 387). In effect, the state performs functions for the maintenance of capitalism, and it plays a part in class struggle on the side of the ruling class. Lenin argues that this applies to all states, including the capitalist democracies.

However, the capitalist democracies do pose a problem for the clarity of Lenin's account of the state. The existence of elections with something approaching universal suffrage suggests that the working class could use its voting strength to take over the state, or at least exert considerable influence on its activities. To take parliamentary democracy seriously, with all its limitations, is to deny that the state is simply an instrument in the hands of the capitalist ruling class. Lenin resolves the difficulty by insisting that parliamentary democracy is a sham: the conditions of electoral struggle are rigged against the interests and representatives of the working class; and, in any case, parliament is not the crucial power within the state, it is just a talking shop. So, even if the first problem could be overcome, the state would still be dominated by the civil and military bureaucracies which do serve the interests of the bourgeoisie. Marxist advocates of a parliamentary road to socialism (most of the West European communist parties, and sections of the non-communist left) tend to accept Lenin's first point, but argue that it can be overcome by the strength of the working class given suitable organization and leadership. On the second point, the claim is that a determined parliament backed by popular support outside parliament can overcome the resistance of the bureaucracy to become the dominant element in the state. Parliamentary democracy is not necessarily a sham, and it involves real advances for the working class.

The disputes within and between these opposed traditions are interminable. Since these disputes turn on differing interpretation of the relation that is supposed to hold in Marxist theory between classes and their interests, on the one hand, and the organizations, institutions, and ideologies of political struggles, on the other, there is no reason to expect that they will ever be resolved. Neither position has proved conspicuously successful in their pursuit of socialism under the political conditions in the capitalist democracies – unless the fact of survival against considerable odds be counted a success. I have discussed these disputes and the weaknesses of both the Leninist and parliamentary road positions in my *Parliamentary Democracy and Socialist Politics* (1983) and there is no need to repeat the argument here. What should be noted here is, first, that the major contributors to these disputes all take classes to be the principal social forces (aided perhaps by such non-class categories as women, youth, ethnic and other minorities), and secondly, that Marxist attempts to take parliamentary democracy seriously and to come to terms with the conditions of electoral politics must reject the analysis of the state as a mere instrument in the hands of the ruling class. In other words, the working class can have an impact on the capitalist state, and on social policy in particular.

THE WELFARE STATE

If the capitalist state is to be analysed in terms of the functional requirements of capitalism and the effects of class struggle, what are we to make of the notion of a 'welfare' state. Gough suggests that the term carries a misleading ideological connotation: it suggests a state concern for the welfare of its citizens and their dependents, opposing the worst distributive effects of market forces. We have seen that some such conception is indeed involved in Marshall's discussion of citizenship and in Titmuss's treatment of the aims of social policy. This is misleading, in Marxist terms, because it presents the state as independent of the functional requirements of capitalism and, at least in its welfare activities, as dominated by ethical considerations. In other words, it gives an idealist gloss on the workings of the state in the societies of advanced capitalism. To avoid that danger Gough proposes to analyse social policy in terms of the requirements of the capitalist economy and the processes of its reproduction: 'For the purposes of this work we shall characterise the welfare state as the use of state power to modify the reproduction of labour power and to maintain the non-working population in capitalist societies (Gough

1979: 44–5). In view of his declared intention of avoiding the pitfalls of Marxist functionalism, this starting point poses an obvious difficulty for Gough's analysis, and it is one that is never satisfactorily overcome.

The reproduction of labour power in Gough's definition refers both to the day-to-day reproduction of the labour power of individual workers, to the rest and recuperation required before they return to work, and to the longer-term reproduction of the labour force as a whole through the entry of new members and departure of the old. Gough also distinguishes between physical and ideological reproduction. There are two basic mechanisms involved in the physical reproduction of labour power. First, wages or salaries are used to purchase consumer goods and services of various kinds. Secondly:

'within the family, a further set of use values is produced, mainly by the housewife and mainly in the form of services: shopping, the preparation of food, . . . Without these services the consumption of commodities purchased in the market is difficult or impossible.'
(*ibid.*: 45)

The state intervenes in both mechanisms: through taxes and benefits which affect disposable incomes; through the direct provision or subsidy of goods and services; through the regulation of household organization, affecting the upbringing of children and the relative positions of men and women. We begin with physical reproduction. In order to account for these interventions, Gough takes his cue from Marx's discussion of the British Factory Acts. Marx argues both that they were the result of working-class struggle and that they served the long-term interests of the capitalist class as a whole by preventing the over-exploitation and exhaustion of the labour force. The legislation was generally opposed by individual capitalists:

'Capital takes no account of the health and length of life of the worker, unless society forces it to do so . . . under free competition, the immanent laws of capitalist production confront the individual capitalist as a coercive force external to him.'
(Marx [1867] 1976: 381; quoted in Gough 1979: 55)

Gough comments as follows:

'The outside intervention of the state was necessary to nullify the

anonymous pressures of the market on each firm. . . . Paradoxically
then, it would appear that labour indirectly aids the long-term
accumulation of capital and strengthens capitalist social relations
by struggling for its own interests within the state. One could
apply this approach to much welfare policy this century.'

(Gough 1979: 55)

State welfare policies may serve the interests of the capitalist class as
a whole even if the capitalists themselves oppose it. Notice how
Gough's 'paradox' overcomes the opposition between functional
explanation and class struggle, but only by subordinating the latter
to the requirements of capital.

Ideological reproduction refers to the reproduction of a labour
force endowed with appropriate knowledge and skills, and with suitable habits of thought and attitudes – deference to proper authority,
regular work habits, and so on. The argument here is that the
continued existence of a labour force endowed with the appropriate
'ideological' characteristics cannot be taken for granted. It is not
an automatic by-product of the existence of capitalist economic relations. One of the major concerns with extensive youth unemployment
in Britain has been the worry that if people don't acquire suitable
habits of work discipline early on, then they may never become reliable
workers. Ideological reproduction is one of the 'requirements' of the
process of capital accumulation.

In his paper 'Ideology and Ideological State Apparatuses' Althusser
suggests that this aspect of reproduction is secured primarily through a
variety of 'ideological state apparatuses', of which education is the
most important in capitalist societies (Althusser 1971). In effect,
education takes people when they are most susceptible and fills them
with a certain amount of knowledge, wrapped up in the ruling
ideology, and it sorts them into categories according to the needs of
the economy: one category, the future workers, leaving compulsory
education at the earliest opportunity, another leaving a few years
later to become white-collar workers and technicians, while the rest
are the future intellectuals, managers, officers, and administrators.

'Each mass ejected *en route* is practically provided with the ideology
which suits the role it has to fulfil in class society: the role of the
exploited (with a "highly developed" "professional", "ethical",

"civic", "national" and a-political consciousness); the role of the
agent of exploitation (ability to give the workers orders and speak
to them: "human relations"), of the agent of repression (ability to
give orders and enforce obedience "without discussion", or ability
to manipulate the demagogy of a political leader's rhetoric), or of
the professional ideologist (ability to treat consciousnesses with
the respect, i.e. with the contempt, blackmail, and demagogy they
deserve, adapted to the accents of Morality, of Virtue, of "Tran-
scendence", of the Nation, of France's World Role, etc.).'

(Althusser 1971: 147)

All of this takes place under the guise of political neutrality: it is run
by professionals, not directly by capitalists or politicians.

Althusser's argument is more complex and sophisticated than the
short account presented here, and this is not the place for a sustained
discussion of his account of ideology (but see Hirst 1979). From the
point of view of the present discussion, the most important point to
notice about Althusser's treatment of education is the way that it is
analysed, not so much as a service to individuals but primarily as a
state service responding to the requirements of capitalist reproduction.
Two problems with this approach should be noted here. First, the
notion of a correspondence between what the educational system
produces and the 'requirements' of the economy raises a host of
(generally unanswered) questions about the mechanisms that operate
to ensure that correspondence (Hussain 1976; Demaine 1981).

In fact, there are problems on both sides of the supposed equation,
problems with the identification of the economy's 'requirements' and
problems with the monitoring and regulation of the performance of
the educational system. There are numerous proposals concerning
what the economy requires of education and how that might be provided, and various bodies engaged in monitoring what educational
institutions do and intervening to change them. These are all subject
to dispute and to the outcomes of political struggles. The 'requirements' of capital accumulation of Gough's functional analysis cannot
be identified with the 'needs' or 'requirements' that are specified
in government policy pronouncements. Regulating the education
system so that it meets what are thought to be the needs of the
economy may or may not be a reasonable objective for governments

to pursue. But there is no reason to suppose that proposals drawn up in such terms, still less those that are finally implemented, are actually determined by the functional 'requirements' of capital accumulation.

This brings us to the second problem; namely, that Althusser's 'point of view of reproduction' opens the door to a Marxist version of sociological functionalism: the ideological state apparatuses exist and do what they do because they have a function to perform. In a postscript Althusser insists on the importance of class struggle, but that merely returns us to the problems of an inconsistent functionalism. If political struggle has consequences that are not determined in advance, then it has consequences for education and other social institutions. It follows that education cannot be analysed as necessarily satisfying the requirements of the economy.

We have already noted this difficulty in relation to Gough's account of social policy in terms of the effects of class struggle and the functional requirements of a capitalist economy. He resolves the tension here by means of the 'paradoxical' suggestion that the results of working-class struggle are to further the long-term interests of capital. It seems that this point applies equally to parliamentary democracy. Thus Gough notes that 'it was fought for by the emerging working class . . . that was long resisted', and goes on to suggest that

'[o]nce universal suffrage and the other major liberal rights are established, this provides a crucial channel through which to obtain welfare improvements. Indeed, welfare becomes a means of integrating the enfranchised working class within the capitalist system and of obtaining certain concessions from the organised labour movement.'   (Gough 1979; 60–1)

Here and elsewhere we are told that reforms resulting from working-class pressure are not working-class victories pure and simple. They may also be means of buying-off discontent. If the interests of capital and the working class are irreconcilable, then the effect of these 'victories' is to disguise the fundamental conflict between them. Or again, the form of welfare provision may be said to reflect the interests of capital. For example, Hall suggests that 'in its effective operations with respect to the popular classes, the state is less and less present as a welfare institution and more and more present as the state of "state monopoly capital" ' (Hall 1979: 18). In this respect he suggests that the anti-state ideology of the radical right may resonate with the experiences of welfare recipients (cf. Leonard 1979). We return to this question in the following chapter.

Finally, if there is an ambiguity in Gough's analysis of the welfare state in terms of both the needs of capital and working-class pressure, there is a corresponding ambiguity over the cuts of the last several years. If the welfare state serves the requirements of capitalist reproduction, then cutbacks may well harm the long-term interests of capital. Because of that ambiguity, Gough concludes:

> 'we would expect to find not so much cuts or a dismantling of the welfare state, but its restructuring. The capitalist state, acting in the interests of its national capital, will seek to alter and adapt social policies to suit the perceived needs of that capital. There will, of course, be disagreement between the various representatives of capitalist interests on what these "needs" are, and different strategies will evolve.'   (Gough 1979: 138)

Notice yet again the inconsistent functionalism of this position. There is a world of difference between the claim that policies are intended to meet the needs of capital and the claim that they meet those needs effectively. If there are different perceptions of the needs of capital and different corresponding strategies for dealing with them, then the strategy that is implemented will be the product of political dispute and conflict. This raises two problems for Gough's analysis. First, if state policies are adopted as the result of political struggle, we cannot also expect them to be determined by the functional needs of capital. If capitalist reproduction depends on state policies, then it has no *autonomous* dynamic. Secondly, if political struggle is accorded a major role in the determination of state welfare (and other) policies, why should the forces engaged in those struggles be identified with classes and class fractions?

POLITICAL FORCES AND FUNCTIONAL ANALYSIS

We have seen that Marxist discussions of the welfare state tend to operate with two conflicting principles of analysis, invoking the supposed functional requirements of a capitalist economy, on the one hand, and the effects of class struggle, on the other. This means that, at their best, Marxist approaches to social policy are often far more sensitive to the complexity of social forces and conditions than many competing analyses. It also mean that they are inconsistent, as we have noted at several points in the preceding discussion. But there are also serious problems with each of the explanatory principles.

The dangers of functional explanation are widely recognized, and Marxist analysis frequently takes steps to avoid it, usually by invoking contradictions or class struggle. Unfortunately, as we have seen, these steps are rarely followed through consistently. All too often Marxist analysis of social policy resorts to the alleged needs of capital accumulation or of the capitalist economy for an important part of its explanation. There are substantial problems here. In particular, the societal mechanisms connecting the alleged need to whatever may be said to serve it remain obscure. This means that the explanation, in terms of the 'requirements' of capital accumulation or whatever, has only a tenuous connection to what it is supposed to explain. If the workings of, say, the education system are to be explained in terms of the satisfaction of certain needs of the capitalist economy, then some account is required of precisely how the education system is compelled to perform that task. Of course, there are influential groups who would like to see education serving what they believe to be the needs of the economy, and some of their proposals influence policies towards educational provision. But if political struggles between competing groups and proposals have any significant role in the determination of educational provision, there is nothing, apart from commitment to functional explanation, that requires us to accept that the policies implemented will have what is said to be the required effect.

As for Marxism's insistence on the role of class struggle, this involves a healthy concern for the explanation of policies in terms of political objectives and struggles. Problems arise with the treatment of those objectives and struggles in class terms, as if the major social forces in a society were classes, or fractions of classes (e.g. finance and industrial capital). The class analysis of politics involves a sociological reductionism in which important elements of political life, if not the whole of it, are treated as if they were given to politics by something outside it, as if they were determined by social or economic conditions quite independently of the activities of parties, the media, trades unions, and other significant political actors. If classes or class fractions really are supposed to be the major political forces in a society, then these other agencies must either be discounted or else reduced to the role of instruments or representatives of the classes themselves. We have already noted a similar reductionism in Goldthorpe's discussion of the British inflation of the 1970s.

The claim that class analysis is often less than helpful for the understanding of political life may well appear perverse in view of what could be seen as the obvious importance of classes in the modern world: the polarizations of interests around the categories of 'capital' and 'labour', the role of socialist and other class-based movements, the Labour parties of Britain and Australasia, the Communist and Social Democratic parties of Western Europe, and so on. The political importance of movements organized, at least in part, around ideas of socialism and claiming to represent the interests of the working class can hardly be denied. What that shows is that there are important cases in which class analysis is employed in the formation and organization of agencies of political struggle and in the mobilization of support around them. It does not establish the theoretical role accorded to the concept of class in Marxist analysis.

I have discussed the dangers of class analysis and its political consequences elsewhere (Hindess 1983), and there is no space to repeat that discussion here. But it is important to be clear what is at stake in the argument that classes should not be considered as political actors. First, to say that classes are not political actors is not at all to deny the significance of cultural divisions or of the distinctions between different categories of economic agent (workers, managers, capitalists, etc.), the reality of strikes, lockouts, rebellions, and other events that are often regarded as instances of class struggle. Nor is it to deny the existence of organized groups claiming to represent classes or sections of them. But it is to say that the analysis of these events as struggles between one class and another class is uninformative. The use of the term 'class struggle' to refer to certain kinds of collective action (strikes, factory occupations, or whatever) obviously requires the existence of classes in the sense of different categories of persons. But it is one thing to analyse a class as a category of persons, and quite another to treat the class itself as a collective actor engaged in struggles with other collective actors.

Secondly, the effect of analysing societies as if classes were the major social actors, even if other categories (women, youth, the bureaucracy, or whatever) are also invoked, is that questions of the conditions of existence of specific parties, movements, and political ideologies, are transformed into questions of the conditions of existence of classes as collective actors. The trouble with that approach, as Marxism has persistently recognized (and equally persistently denied) is that classes do not directly present themselves as actors in political life. To examine political struggles is to find state apparatuses, political parties, factions, and other organizations, demonstrations, riotous mobs, magazines and newspapers, and so on, but it is not to find classes as such lined up against each other. Nor is it to find that the issues at stake are readily translatable into direct conflicts between the working class and the bourgeoisie for political hegemony.

To treat the forces engaged in promoting social change (say the institution of the NHS in 1947), or in preventing it, as if they were classes is at best allegorical – the narrative treatment of one subject under the guise of another having similarities to it – and at worst thoroughly misleading. Political analysis does frequently take the allegorical form of treating complex patterns of collective actions as if they were the actions of, for example, a nation, a class or an electorate. The allegorical analysis of politics in class terms would then be a matter of narrative convention rather than a strict reductionism, an expository device that may have to be relinquished on more detailed inspection. Unfortunately, the undoubted gain in narrative simplicity is bought at a heavy cost in terms of intellectual rigour and effective political analysis.

VIII

Liberalism

In his postscript to *The Constitution of Liberty*, 'Why I am not a Conservative', Hayek notes that 'what I have called "liberalism" has little to do with any political movement that goes under that name today' (Hayek 1960: 408). In continental Europe it stands more for 'a desire to impose upon the world a preconceived rational pattern than to provide opportunity for free growth. The same is largely true of what has called itself Liberalism in England at least since the time of Lloyd George' (*ibid.*: 408). Liberalism is a complex set of traditions of social thought, but for the purposes of this book we use the terms 'liberal' and 'liberalism' in something like Hayek's sense to refer, not to the doctrines of the British Liberal Party, but rather to a body of political thought 'concerned mainly with limiting the coercive powers of all government' (*ibid.*: 103) in the interests of liberty and a free society. There are of course interpretations of the liberal tradition and of liberty other than the one we consider here. In *Taking Rights Seriously*, for example, Dworkin treats 'the liberal concept of equality' (Dworkin 1977: 273) as fundamental, arguing that the rights to particular liberties may be derived from it. Or, again, Plant maintains that Hayek's rejection of equality in the name of liberty is disingenuous, and that greater equality is to be seen as a means to greater liberty (Plant 1984). The centrality of the concern for liberty in the liberalism of Hayek and others means that liberal political analysis operates very differently from that of the Marxism considered in Chapter VII above. Marxism operates with a relatively systematic theory of social structure and social change, and it aims at bringing about definite changes in the class structure of capitalist societies. Liberalism's interest in social structure is rather different: it is important primarily because of its consequences for the liberty of the individual. Liberals certainly have things to say about structural features of social relations, but there is not the same concern to develop a systematic account of the structure of society as a whole. We shall see that liberalism and Marxism share a tendency to essentialize the operations of 'the market', but they arrive at that essentialism in different ways.

Since we are concerned with contemporary approaches to the analysis of social policy, our interest lies in contemporary liberalism rather than its nineteenth-century predecessors. This 'liberalism' may not be associated with a movement of that name, but it is now strongly represented in British politics by important elements in the Conservative Party, the 'independent' Institute of Economic Affairs, and other organizations. There is a good general survey of current liberal views on social and economic policy in Bosanquet's *After the New Right* (1983). This chapter concentrates on the work of Hayek and Friedman and on recent publications of the Institute of Economic Affairs (IEA) devoted specifically to the British welfare state. Of course, these different positions are not equivalent. The IEA publishes tracts of a broadly 'liberal' character, but it is not identified with any one position within that perspective. Hayek may be misguided, but he is also careful and systematic. The same can hardly be said of Friedman, at least in his ventures outside the realm of technical economics – and even within that realm, serious doubts have been raised about the technical quality of some of his most influential work on inflation and the money supply (Hendry and Ericsson 1983). If nothing else, discussion of his work will show that academic prominence is no guarantee of quality of argument.

But in all cases, we find a marked hostility to the welfare state, which, at least in its current extension, is said to be oppressive, inefficient, and unpopular. The point is forcefully made in the deliberate play on words in a recent IEA title. *Over-Ruled on Welfare* (Harris and Seldon 1979) tries to show both that public expenditure on the provision of services in Britain goes against popular wishes and that it involves excessive state control – hence the public are overruled in two senses. This liberalism is therefore concerned to restrict the activities of the state, and in the case of social policy, to replace them by market-based services, private philanthropy, and minimal state provision for those in real need. We begin by considering the liberal case for markets and then move on to their views on minimal government and the rule of law, and their implications for the analysis of social policy, before concluding with some more general critical comments.

THE CASE FOR MARKETS

A distinctive feature of contemporary liberal discussion of economic and social policy is the claim that state intervention is generally a bad thing in that it distorts the operations of markets, it rarely achieves the desired results, and it reduces the liberty of the individual. In fact, that claim is generally qualified. Liberalism is not opposed to the existence of governments, but it does hope to minimize their effects on liberty and the market by means of the constraints which Hayek describes in terms of the rule of law. We return to these qualifications below, but to show their significance it may be helpful to begin with the crude liberal case for the market presented in the Friedmans' *Free to Choose* (1980).

Friedman

The book begins with a tendentious account of a political and economic miracle in the late-nineteenth-century USA, and to a lesser extent Britain, that was based on two sets of ideas. These are first, Adam Smith's notion of the 'hidden hand', indicating the capacity of the free market to co-ordinate self-interested activities towards the common good, and secondly, the idea of political freedom exemplified in the American Declaration of Independence. Unfortunately, we are told, recent years have seen a spectacular increase in government interventions, more so in Britain than the USA. These are based on good intentions and on self-interest, but they have had unfortunate economic effects, and they have endangered freedom. In effect, we have moved a long way towards socialism. Happily there is still time to reverse that drift. To see why we should do so it is necessary to understand the two ideas noted above. *Free to Choose* is therefore a polemic in favour of the market and what Friedman understands by freedom.

We begin with the market. The argument here turns on a contrast between two ways of co-ordinating the activities of large numbers of people: command and voluntary co-operation, the primary example of the latter being the market. All social life depends on both these methods, but it is only where markets predominate that we find both freedom and prosperity. The most important feature of the market is that it involves voluntary exchanges of goods and services between individuals. Since it is voluntary, exchange will take place only if both parties believe that they will benefit from it. This may seem plausible in the case of two individuals, but what happens if there are millions of individuals and thousands of things to exchange?

What happens is that the price mechanism extends the principle of voluntary exchange to large numbers, thereby allowing widespread co-operation without central direction. The price mechanism works wonders, and it does so because prices perform three functions that are essential to a system of widespread voluntary co-operation: they provide information on what goods and services are available, and what they can be exchanged for; they provide incentives, because the pattern of prices indicates those goods and services where demand exceeds supply; and, finally, they distribute income (what people get in exchange for what they can sell). Because prices do all of these things, it follows that any attempt to interfere with one function must have consequences for the others. For example, government interference with the distribution of income (on the grounds, say, of social justice) will also interfere with the other two functions. It will artificially increase some incentives and reduce others (e.g. the incentive to work), distort the information carried by prices, and make the workings of economic life generally less efficient. The claim is not then that prices invariably perform the functions just listed, but rather that they will do so in the absence of market distortions.

We shall see that this simple view of the effects of markets requires considerable qualification. For the moment, notice that Friedman's treatment of markets and the price mechanism pays little attention to institutional conditions. Consider, for example, the shift from voluntary exchange between two individuals to the price mechanism linking millions:

'if an exchange between two parties is voluntary, it will not take place unless both believe they will benefit from it. . . . This key insight is obvious for a simple exchange between two individuals.

It is far more difficult to understand how it can enable people living all over the world to cooperate to promote their separate interests. The price system is the mechanism that performs this task without central direction, without requiring people to speak to one another or to like one another. . . . As a result, the price system enables people to cooperate peacefully in one phase of their life while each one goes about his business in respect of everything else.'

(Friedman and Friedman 1980: 31–2)

Why should we assume that the price system promotes the interests of 'people living all over the world', irrespective of the institutional conditions in which it operates? We considered one instance of the more general claim that the effects of prices are a consequence of institutional conditions in Chapter VII. Marxism interprets the price system (including wages as the prices for labour services) as the crucial mechanism of the exploitation of the working class by the capitalist class. Here the appearance of voluntary exchange masks an underlying exploitative relationship. On that view it is impossible to analyse the consequences of prices independently of the character of property relations. It is not necesary to endorse the Marxist analysis of exploitation to see that Friedman's simplistic account of the beneficial effects of prices need not be accepted without question.

Or again, there is a curious circularity in Friedman's discussion of the workings of the price mechanism, as if the distribution of resources had no bearing on the formation of prices and their effects. If two individuals endowed with a given set of preferences and resources enter freely into an exchange, then each gets something they want and so each benefits. In effect, the preferences that people have in a market situation are used as a measure of the success of the market in catering for those preferences. But as soon as we notice that people's preferences are, at least in part, a function of the choices open to them, then that justification of the market appears entirely circular. Here, too, the point is not necessarily to argue against markets as a mode of distribution, but rather to insist that their consequences cannot be considered independently of the institutional conditions (in this case the distribution of property and other resources) in which they operate. We return to the distribution of resources in a moment.

In fact, apart from polemics against government and trades unions, Friedman has almost nothing to say about institutional conditions. One respect in which institutional conditions might be thought to have changed significantly since the nineteenth century is the extent to which economic activity is dominated by large corporations. He tells us that the distribution of income through the market is determined by the difference between a person's receipts from the sale of goods and services and the costs of producing them:

'the existence of the modern corporation does not alter matters. We speak loosely of the "corporation's income" or of "business" having an income. That is figurative language. The corporation is an intermediary between its owners – the stockholders – and the resources other than the stockholders' capital, the services of which it purchases. Only people have incomes and they derive them through the market from the resources they own.'

(*ibid.*: 40)

Friedman is mistaken about the legal standing of the corporation. The corporation is a legal person distinct from its stockholders, and it is the owner of its assets (Hadden 1977; Cutler *et al.* 1977, Ch. 11). But the main points to notice here are first that Friedman's account allows him to dispense with what many have thought to be the problems posed by the power of the large corporation – they are only intermediaries – and secondly, that he can treat restrictions on corporations as if they were really restrictions on human individuals. For example, in Chapter 2, 'The Tyranny of Controls', he gives examples of business executives afraid to speak out against government controls:

'Tongue-lashed by Senator Henry Jackson for earning "obscene profits", not a single member of a group of oil industry executives answered back, or even left the room and refused to submit to further personal abuse. Oil company executives, who in private express strong opposition to the present complex structure of federal controls . . . or to the major extension of government intervention proposed by President Carter, make bland public statements approving the objectives of the controls.'

(*ibid.*: 91)

Here the fact or the threat of government controls over the behaviour of corporations is presented as a major attack on the freedom of speech of human individuals. No doubt, the executives Friedman describes felt they had good pragmatic reasons for their behaviour. So do the many employees who have to suffer abuse from their superiors without answering back. It is significant that Friedman treats the first situation as a threat to freedom of speech, but not the second. The reason, of course, is clear: employees are always free to resign and seek work elsewhere if they don't like their conditions of appointment. Controls in the workplace are a consequence of exchanges freely entered into by employees and employer (acting as intermediary for the stockholders), but controls by government are imposed. By treating the corporation as a mere intermediary, Friedman extends a defence of private property in the name of individual freedom to a defence of the large corporation against public controls. We will return to this point.

Finally, let us return to the distribution of resources. In Friedman's account this is not an issue requiring systematic analysis; it is the result of chance and choice. Chance determines our genetic endowment, family background, inherited resources, and so on:

> 'But choice also plays an important role. Our decisions about how to use our resources, whether to work hard or take it easy, to enter one occupation or another, to engage in one venture or another, to save or spend – these may determine whether we dissipate our resources or improve and add to them.'
>
> (*ibid.*: 41)

So, immediately after dissolving the problem of large corporations, Friedman goes on to reduce other institutional conditions of economic life to some combination of choice and chance. In effect, Friedman's social analysis reduces to three interacting elements: human individuals making choices, governments interfering, and chance. If that simplistic social analysis is acceptable, then much of the rest of his argument will seem entirely plausible.

Hayek

It is all too easy to pick holes in Friedman's social theory. But there is a more serious strand of contemporary liberalism, represented particularly in the works of Hayek, in which many of Friedman's crude simplicities are retained, but only with significant qualifications. The effect of these qualifications is to avoid some of the grosser features of Friedman's position but without always avoiding the problems posed by his neglect of institutional conditions. Hayek's treatment of the market as a spontaneous social order allows him to advance two lines of argument against government planning, one concerning the epistemological difficulties of any central plan and the other involving particular conceptions of freedom and coercion. We begin with the notion of spontaneous social order.

Hayek notes that there are many features of orderly social activity that are the results of human actions, and therefore of intentions, but not of any single plan. In any society its language, law, and custom have this character, and so in general do markets:

> 'Much of the opposition to a system of freedom under general laws arises from the inability to conceive of an effective co-ordination of human activities without deliberate organization by a commanding intelligence. One of the achievements of economic theory has been to explain how such a mutual adjustment of the spontaneous activities of individuals is brought about by the market, provided that there is a known delimitation of the sphere of control of each individual.'
>
> (Hayek 1960: 159)

We shall see below that Hayek introduces qualifications which seriously undermine the force of this assertion. For the moment, notice that the market is presented as a form of ordered social activity 'without deliberate organization by a commanding intelligence' (*ibid.*: 154). But there is a further sense in which the market is an example of spontaneous social order. This is that only part of the knowledge involved in the processes of mutual adjustment is fully conscious:

> 'man's mind is itself a product of the civilization in which he has grown up and . . . it is unaware of much of the experience which has shaped it – experience that assists it by being embodied in the habits, conventions, language and moral beliefs which are part of its makeup.'
>
> (*ibid.*: 24)

The knowledge involved in the workings of the market and other spontaneous orders is therefore dispersed amongst numerous individuals, and much of it is not consciously formulated. Hayek therefore argues that the orderliness of the market 'involving an adjustment to circumstances, knowledge of which is dispersed among a great many people, cannot be established by central direction' (*ibid.*: 160).

We therefore have what amounts to an epistemological argument for the inevitable failure of planning: planning cannot replicate the orderly mutual adjustment of the market because it can never marshall all the required knowledge in one place. Hayek elaborated this and other arguments in the 1930s in his attempts to demonstrate the impossibility of socialist economic planning – and there can be little doubt that the argument is effective against certain utopian conceptions of what planning might be able to achieve. We return to this question in Chapter IX. In *The Road to Serfdom* (1944), and many subsequent writings, he uses this 'epistemological' argument to show that, even with the best of intentions, the attempt at central planning leads inexorably to totalitarianism: the plan fails, and this is attributed not to the impossibility of planning in general but rather to the weakness of the plan in question and inadequacy of its control mechanisms; a more comprehensive plan is introduced which also (inevitably) fails, leading to yet more ambitious planning, and so on. In this perspective there can be no half-way house between the market and a planned society. Central planning is dangerous, and it is to be avoided like the plague.

Central planning is to be avoided therefore, not only because it is ineffective but also because of its consequences for liberty. What Hayek understands by 'freedom' is the 'state in which a man is not subject to coercion by the arbitrary will of another or others' (Hayek 1960: 11). It may not be possible to eliminate coercion entirely, but the aim of liberalism should be to reduce it to a minimum. Hayek devotes the first chapter of *The Constitution of Liberty* (1960) to distinguishing this from alternative conceptions of liberty. This is not the place for a discussion of the different meanings of liberty, but it is worth noting two points. First, one alternative conception of liberty is clearly represented in Orwell's review of *The Road to Serfdom*: 'But he does not see, or will not admit, that return to a "free" competition means for the great mass of people a tyranny probably worse, because more irresponsible, than that of the State' (Orwell [1944] 1968: 143). Orwell has in mind the 'tyranny' of an unregulated economy, the effects of slumps and mass unemployment. The liberal response is straightforward: unemployment is indeed a misfortune, and it does limit what a person might realistically choose to do, but it is not coercion. Underlying Orwell's objection is the view that freedom may be constrained by impersonal economic and social conditions, as well as by the deliberate actions of other individuals. We shall see later that Barbara Wootton employs such a conception of freedom to great effect in *Freedom Under Planning* (1945), her response to *The Road to Serfdom*.

Secondly, Hayek discusses liberty and coercion largely in the context of relations between the state and its citizens, as if a reduction in coercion by the state is equivalent to a reduction in coercion *per se*. This is misleading since, as Weber points out in his discussion of law in *Economy and Society*, the reduction of legal constraints on economic activity operates primarily for the advantage of the economically powerful (Weber 1968: esp. 729f.). The fact that employees are not legally prevented from resigning and seeking alternative employment does not mean that they are not subject to coercion by their employers. The extension of freedom of contract in a society may well go hand in hand with the development of highly authoritarian relationships in the sphere of employment. We noted a similar blind spot in Friedman's treatment of government controls over corporate behaviour.

But, to return to the market, why should we regard it as a desirable social order? 'The orderliness of social activity shows itself in the fact that the individual can carry out a consistent plan of action that, at almost every stage, rests on the expectation of certain contributions from his fellows' (Hayek 1960: 159–60). Short of total collapse, all social life is orderly in that sense. To claim that much for the market, and no more, is really to claim very little. Booms, slumps, wild inflation and massive unemployment are all entirely compatible with the orderliness of markets – and much of the case for central government intervention comes from a desire to avoid these more extreme fluctuations. When Hayek praises the market for its capacity to realize 'an effective co-ordination of human activities' (Hayek 1960) there is more at stake than orderliness in this limited sense. For Hayek, as for Friedman, markets work well only under the appropriate institutional conditions. What Hayek has to offer in this respect is more sophisticated than Friedman's simplistic account of governments interfering, individual choice, and chance, but it is not without serious problems.

One of the conditions required for the proper operation of markets is what Hayek calls 'the rule of law', which constrains the forms of government intervention in social and economic activity. We consider the rule of law below. For the rest we must return to the notion of *spontaneous* social order. We have seen that in this context spontaneity involves, first, the use of knowledge that is not consciously formulated and, secondly, the absence of a controlling centre. Does the lack of a controlling centre mean that anything goes, that individuals can pursue whatever desires happen to enter their heads – and that everything will still be effectively co-ordinated by Smith's 'hidden hand'? Not at all: 'The Scottish theorists were very much aware how delicate this artificial structure of civilization was which rested on man's more primitive and ferocious instincts being tamed and checked by institutions he neither designed nor could control' (*ibid.*: 60). Hayek goes on to insist on the importance of tradition for a free society, and further, 'that freedom has never worked without deeply ingrained moral beliefs and that coercion can be reduced to a minimum only where individuals can be expected as a rule to conform voluntarily to certain principles (*ibid.*: 62).

So, the effective workings of the market depend on the existence of appropriate traditions and on the moral behaviour of capitalists (and others) in the market-place. There is an interesting discussion of the implications of that point in *Social Limits to Growth* (1976) by Fred Hirsch. In Hayek's account it is clear that much of the necessary tradition and morality must be poorly understood since it is embedded in knowledge that is not consciously formulated. So, it is not the market as such that defines a desirable social order but rather the market operating under moral and traditional constraints that cannot be clearly specified.

This difficulty over 'the market' is compounded if we consider the other difficulty we noted with regard to Friedman's discussion of institutional conditions; namely, his treatment of the corporation as a mere intermediary between stockholders and others. Consider

Hayek's discussion in 'The Corporation in a Democratic Society'. His position is more complex than Friedman's, but it is not without its own serious problems. Hayek's thesis is:

> 'if we want to limit the powers of corporations to where they are beneficial, we shall have to confine them much more than we have yet done to one specific goal, that of the profitable use of the capital entrusted to the management by the stockholders.'
>
> (Hayek 1967: 300)

Hayek makes some proposals that he believes might help to bring about this desirable state of affairs. We may have reservations about Hayek's claim that the single-minded pursuit of profit by corporations to the exclusion of all other concerns is the most beneficial option for the rest of us, and we may note that the pursuit of profit can give corporations powerful reasons for concerning themselves with the political complexions of governments in the economies in which they operate. But what is most significant for present purposes is Hayek's recognition that corporations do not presently restrict their activities strictly to what he regards as the profitable use of their stockholders' capital – if they did so, there would be little point in proposing that their activities should be confined in that way. Where Friedman treats corporations as nothing but intermediaries, Hayek says that is what they should be, thereby admitting that they are not. Corporations, and therefore the markets that they play any significant part in, do not operate as Hayek would wish. In effect, corporations are significant economic actors distinct from their stockholders, and Hayek wishes things were otherwise. Perhaps his primary concern is that their use of resources for ends other than long-run profit maximization is an invitation for public control: 'Unless we believe that the corporations serve the public interest best by devoting their resources to the single aim of securing the largest return in terms of long-run profits, the case for private enterprise breaks down' (*ibid*.: 312). Since, on Hayek's own account, corporations already go beyond that aim, the case for public regulation is clear. There are two points to notice here about Hayek's treatment of corporations. First, it is a well-known pluralist argument that the economic autonomy of large numbers of individuals is a condition of political freedom and democracy. But, as the American pluralist Robert Dahl shows in his

A Preface to Economic Democracy (1985), it does not follow that modern forms of corporate property can be defended on such grounds. Unlike Friedman, Hayek at least recognizes that there is a problem here. Secondly, his case against political control does not rest on any reasoned assessment of how existing corporations could be expected to behave in its absence, but rather on an act of blind faith.

Hayek's case for 'the market' is by no means as clear-cut as it first appears. What he presents in his account of the market as a spontaneous social order, and again in discussion of the corporation, is a liberal utopia which, as it happens, we do not inhabit. It is not a case for just any old market, but rather for a market in which corporations are nothing but the agents of their stockholders' interests and which operates under 'the rule of law' and is governed by suitable traditions and moral beliefs. In fact, on Hayek's own account, governments go beyond the bounds of the rule of law, and corporations do not behave as they should. As for appropriate traditions and moral beliefs, in their absence (and even in their presence) they cannot be fully understood, and they could not be imposed by central control if they were understood. The general liberal case for 'liberalizing' our present cluster of public regulation and provision and relying on the market as much as possible is entirely a matter of faith. The Hayekian liberal has no shortage of excuses if things go wrong.

MINIMAL GOVERNMENT AND THE RULE OF LAW

Contemporary liberalism is sometimes presented as if it were a doctrine of minimal government, but in Hayek's view at least, this is misleading:

> 'though a few theorists have demanded that the activities of government should be limited to the maintenance of law and order, such a stand cannot be justified by the principle of liberty. Only the coercive measures of government need be strictly limited.'
>
> (Hayek 1960: 257)

Liberals are not necessarily opposed to governments concerning themselves with economic affairs or social welfare. What matters from this point of view is not so much the extent of government

activity but rather its character. There are many reasons why a
liberal may wish to oppose government social or economic policy.
Some of these are a matter of principle, raising issues of coercion and
the rule of law. Some are to do with the supposed practical effects of
excessive reliance on government action as a means of promoting the
welfare of individuals and interest groups. Finally, there are reasons
to do with consideration of the effectiveness or otherwise of the
policy in question. There is a clear general argument of this kind
in the 'epistemological' case for markets and against planning discussed above. If much of the knowledge involved in economic activity
is dispersed and not consciously formulated, then, Hayek argues,
governments are not well placed to direct the economic activities of
particular individuals. Quite apart from any considerations of individual liberty, there are, from this point of view, good practical
reasons why governments should stick to laying down general rules
rather than intervening in particular cases. In this section we concentrate on the other two sets of reasons, beginning with the rule
of law.

The rule of law

Hayek interprets the rule of law as referring to an ideal condition in
which all government actions are bound by general rules that are fixed
and announced beforehand. We consider a different interpretation
in a moment. Hayek's ideal is one that can never be entirely realized
in practice, but it does provide him with a fundamental standard
against which all governments (however democratic) and their policies
(however popular) can and must be measured. The rules must be
general in the sense that they are not aimed at the needs, wants, or
activities of particular people. Rather, they should identify circumstances in which government would use its coercive powers. The
individuals against whom those powers might be used are just those
who infringe the general rules; they should not be identified in any
other way. Since the point is to restrain the coercive activities of
government, these general rules should not be framed so as to
discriminate either against or in favour of any group of persons
known in advance – against Jews or Blacks, for example. Laws against
speeding lay down general rules of this kind: they apply equally to

all motorists, and they do not single out particular individuals (say, BMW drivers) for special attention. Retrospective legislation is likely to violate the rule of law on this interpretation since its victims and beneficiaries usually can be identified in advance.

General rules of this kind that are announced in advance are a defence against the arbitrary actions of governments. They are necessary in Hayek's view both for the proper working of the market and for the existence of liberty precisely because they allow individuals to plan their affairs secure in the knowledge that government powers will not be used deliberately to frustrate their efforts. Once governments go beyond the enforcement of certain general rules, their activities inevitably involve the coercion of particular individuals. Since general rules of the kind Hayek favours are not aimed to produce particular effects on particular people, their precise consequences cannot be known in advance. They provide a framework for the decisions and actions of individuals, but they do not determine what those decisions and actions will be. From this point of view there is no reason in principle why governments should not concern themselves with the regulation of economic affairs. But their interventions should take the form of a framework of laws within which markets can operate, rather than the direction of economic activity by a central authority.

Here and elsewhere, Hayek discusses government social and economic policy as if interference with market operations inevitably involves the infringement of liberty. It is not clear why that should be the case. Consider the example raised by Pigou in his review of *The Road to Serfdom* (Pigou 1944). The wartime practice of directing particular individuals into specific jobs is an infringement of liberty that may be defended for a limited period on the grounds of national emergency. Pigou argues that Hayek fails to distinguish between that practice and the state's

> 'determining the number of persons to be admitted into different occupations, and securing this number by manipulating rates of pay, and so on. In the former case individual liberty is, of course, directly attacked; but in the latter are individuals really less free than they would be if the numbers to be admitted into different occupations were determined by the play of the market?'
>
> (Pigou 1944: 218)

In this example, the occupational choices of individuals are certainly constrained as a result of government policy. But, from the point of view of those affected, the manner in which they are constrained is no different from the effects of market forces. It seems then that government interference in markets is to count as a coercive infringement of liberty, whether or not it is experienced as such by the individuals concerned.

Similar considerations apply to the welfare state. It is entirely proper for governments to be concerned with the welfare of their citizens, provided only that their welfare activities are constrained by the rule of law. The difficulty in discussing 'the welfare state', in Hayek's view, is that the term has no clear meaning. Some of the activities normally included under that heading are unobjectionable and may even 'make a free society more attractive, others are incompatible with it' (Hayek 1960: 259). For this reason Hayek is not opposed to the welfare state as such, and he tends to favour state involvement in limited areas of welfare. For example, there are cases where it may be in the interests of all members of the community that there be public provision of amenities such as parks, museums, and some kinds of sports facilities. Or again, governments in all the economically advanced societies have concerned themselves with health and education, and with some level of provision for the indigent and disabled.

Such concerns are not necessarily illegitimate, provided that their pursuit does not involve the adoption of coercive powers by government. Unfortunately, the welfare state is not always so benign: there are welfare objectives whose pursuit inevitably conflicts with the rule of law, and coercive measures are sometimes introduced in pursuit of otherwise legitimate objectives. On the second point, for example, we have noted that governments may concern themselves with the provision of health services, education, and a variety of amenities. In many cases governments provide these services directly. We shall see that liberals have reasons to question the wisdom of relying on government for the provision of such services because of doubts about their efficiency or effectiveness, but they do not necessarily regard them as an infringement of liberty. Liberty is threatened not by government provision of services but rather by its claim to the exclusive right to provide them. State provision of health or education services may be more or less effective, but it is a threat to liberty only if their use is made compulsory. Where state services are provided, it should be possible for market-based provision to develop alongside them. This is not to say that there should be no public regulation of private services, only that the standards applied to them should apply equally to the public services themselves.

The other respect in which the activities of the welfare state may be a cause for concern in Hayek's view is that the pursuit of some kinds of welfare objectives inevitably undermine the rule of law. Consider the question of security against the risks of ill health, injury, or unemployment, or against the consequences of old age. Here government may well be able to reduce these risks or help people to provide for them:

> 'however, an important distinction has to be drawn between two conceptions of security: a limited security which can be achieved for all and which is, therefore, no privilege, and absolute security, which in a free society cannot be achieved for all. The first of these is . . . the assurance of a given minimum of sustenance for all; and the second is the assurance of a given standard of life, which is determined by comparing the standard enjoyed by a person or group with that of others.'
>
> (*ibid.*: 259)

There are, of course, problems about what the minimum standard should be and the conditions under which it should be provided. In his earlier discussion of these issues in *The Road to Serfdom* Hayek goes on to suggest that 'there is particularly the important question whether those who thus rely on the community should indefinitely enjoy all the same liberties as the rest' (Hayek 1944: 90). There is no question here of social policy operating to secure that equality of citizenship which plays such an important part in Marshall's account of the welfare state.

The second kind of security raises considerations of what a person deserves, and therefore questions of distributive justice. Hayek does not object to government involvement in welfare activities, but he does object in principle to 'the kind of welfare state that aims at "social justice" and becomes "primarily a redistributor of income". It is bound to lead back to socialism and its essentially coercive and arbitrary methods' (Hayek 1960: 260). The pursuit of 'social' or 'distributive' justice inevitably conflicts with the rule of law. It aims to secure for sections of the population a level of income and standard of living which they could not or do not secure for themselves through the exchange of services in the market. Public policy must therefore discriminate to the advantage of some and the disadvantage of others, with the result that citizens are no longer equally subject to the same general rules. On similar grounds it could be argued that the exercise of administrative discretion conflicts with the requirement that the same general rules should apply to all. The pursuit of social justice or the attempt to tailor social-policy provision to the specific needs of individuals undermines the rule of law. Hayek's objection to the pursuit of social justice does not involve the view that market outcomes are *just*. The point rather is that any attempt to alter market outcomes after the event in the name of social justice (or anything else) is an attack on the rule of law and an infringement of liberty.

What is it about Hayek's account of the rule of law that leads him to this conclusion? This is not the place to consider the debates around the notion of the rule of law. For present purposes it is sufficient to consider the rather different account by Roscoe Pound in his article 'Rule of Law' in *The International Encyclopaedia of the Social Sciences* (1934). Pound describes the rule of law as:

> 'a characteristic doctrine of the common law that the judiciary, in ordinary legal proceedings, may pronounce upon the legal validity of the acts of the king's ministers and servants and hence, in the United States, upon the validity of administrative, executive and legislative action with reference to the constitution and, in the case of administrative and executive action, the statutes governing such action.'

> (Pound 1934: 463)

Here the decisive consideration concerns the practical possibility of judicial review of administrative and executive action, and therefore the existence of a framework of laws and institutional conditions in which such reviews can take place. In terms of that consideration the rule of law is limited, in Britain, by the doctrine of the supremacy of Parliament, and in Britain and the USA, by the existence of a considerable area of non-reviewable administrative discretion.

The contrast with Hayek's account of the rule of law is instructive. The importance of judicial review in Pound's account is that it grounds the rule of law in social practices and institutional conditions rather than in a wholly abstract relation between government action and certain principles. There is nothing in the idea that the legality of government action should be subject to judicial review to rule out government interference with the operations of markets, the pursuit of social justice, the exercise of administrative discretion, and other practices to which Hayek objects. The central concern of Hayek's account is not so much the institutional conditions which make possible judicial review of government action, but rather the sub-ordination of government action to certain general principles. The rule of law means simply that the liberty of the individual, as Hayek understands it, must take priority over all other concerns and objectives. Why the liberty of the individual should be accorded quite that status is a question to which we return in the concluding chapter.

The irresponsibility of government

The final set of liberal arguments against government spending on the provision of services to be considered here concern the alleged irresponsibility of government. The point is neatly made in the title of the IEA pamphlet *Over-Ruled on Welfare*. Harris and Seldon suggest that the British public's preference for choice in education and medicine has been frustrated by 'representative' government. In fact, they argue, government provision has been a major obstacle to higher standards: 'In education and health, the false – because unrealised and unrealisable – claim of equal standards for all stands in 1979 as the main barrier to better standards for all' (Harris and Seldon 1979: 185). This outcome is not accidental, nor is it the result of peculiar features of the British situation. It is a consequence of the choice of government as opposed to market provision. Critics of the market and others who favour state intervention in social welfare often refer to market imperfections as one of the reasons for government intervention. It may be claimed, for example, that commercial activities often create costs for third parties (air and water pollution, noise and vibration from heavy lorries, etc.), that there are dangers of monopolistic or oligopolistic supply, or that market provision of health or education will result in the poor getting a bad deal. The argument then is that state intervention is required in order to prevent or counter such imperfections.

Harris and Seldon respond in two ways. First, they assert that market imperfections are often the result of government action or inaction (e.g. their failure to curb the power of trades unions), and that in any case government remedies are often worse than the disease. Secondly, they suggest that the case for government intervention ignores the fact of government imperfections. The poor may get a bad deal from market provision but, as we saw in Chapter VI, they get a bad deal from state provision too. Harris and Seldon therefore argue that market imperfection supports a case for its replacement by government provision only if it can be shown that government provision would do better. This, of course, they deny.

What then are the liberal objections to public provision? We have considered two kinds of objection already. One is the alleged threat to liberty noted above. The other is the argument discussed in Chapter V that the assumption of government responsibility for welfare leads to a widespread scramble by particular interests for public support with damaging consequences for the interests of all. What is at issue at this point is the more mundane question of the practical consequences of government attempts at provision. The liberal argument is that government provision is generally irresponsible: it is not sensitive to the needs of those to whom services should be supplied, and what it provides is not what the electorate desires.

On the first point, the argument is straightforward. The market is sensitive to people's needs in a way that bureaucratic provision cannot be. Since market exchanges take place only if both parties believe they can benefit from the exchange, it follows, first, that suppliers can survive only if they provide their customers with what they want, and secondly, that unsatisfied customers provide an opportunity for others to profit. For this reason:

'the economic market is superior to the political ballot-box in its ability to cater sensitively for minorities . . . . Small groups of

customers with unusual needs or preferences can invariably find a
supplier to meet their distinctive requirements at a price.'

(ibid.: 68)

Within the state system, on the other hand, people have to pay for
services, through taxation, 'whether they are satisfied with them or
not' (*ibid.*: 74). Not only is there no incentive for the state system to
respond to clients' needs, but the level of taxation makes it impossible
for unsatisfied customers to seek satisfaction elsewhere. The implication is clear: if only the state would get off the tax-payers' back,
then the market would provide for those needs which state services
currently satisfy more or less badly. What is at stake here is an
argument about choice, to which we return in a moment, and a view
of taxation as a form of coercion which should be kept to an absolute
minimum. Friedman presents this view of taxation as follows:

> 'An essential part of economic freedom is freedom to choose how to
> use our income: how much to spend on ourselves and on what
> items; how much to save and in what form; how much to give
> away and to whom. Currently, more than 40 per cent of our
> income is disposed of on our behalf by government. . . . One of us
> once suggested a new national holiday, 'Personal Independence
> Day' – that day in the year when we stop working to pay the
> expenses of government . . . and start working to pay for the items
> we . . . choose in the light of our own needs and desires.'

(Friedman 1980: 89)

There are two points to notice here: first, the claim that taxation is
an imposition on individual freedom, and secondly, the suggestion
that the level of taxation is a measure of that imposition. On the
second point, Friedman's presentation is, to say the least, disingenuous. Wage and salary negotiations normally take place in the
context of a prevailing level of taxation. For incomes resulting from
employment (the vast majority) it is generally post-tax income that
is relevant to the issues of economic freedom raised in Friedman's
first sentence. There is certainly no reason to suppose that incomes
before tax would remain at the same level if we had a significantly
lower level of taxation. Given the prevailing level of taxation, then,
the differential treatment of individuals on the same income (because of
tax relief on mortgage interest, dependants' allowances, or whatever)

may still require some justification. But to question such differences is not to question the prevailing level of taxation itself. The case is rather different for unearned incomes, but even there investment decisions by private individuals or pension funds will be made in the light of prevailing taxes. Taxation is, of course, an imposition on the collective labour and wealth of society, but much state activity makes a contribution to that collective labour and wealth. It is seriously misleading to present the level of taxation as a measure of government constraint on individual freedom. To make this point is not to say that there is nothing wrong with the present system of taxation. Nor is it to say that there might not be good reasons for objecting to the overall level of taxation – but it is to say that Friedman's reason is not one of them.

Returning now to the more general claim, why *should* taxation be seen as an unjustified imposition on individual freedom? The Friedmans present the issue in terms of freedom, but a rather different version of the claim that taxation is theft can be found in Robert Nozick's *Anarchy, State and Utopia*: 'Individuals have rights, and there are things no person or group may do to them (without violating those rights)' (Nozick 1974: ix). In particular, individuals have rights to the use and disposal of the fruits of their own labour. From this point of view, personal taxation would seem to be a violation of individual rights. In fact, both Nozick and the Friedmans would regard as defensible the level of taxation required to finance the activities of a minimal state, national defence, the maintenance of law and order, the enforcement of contracts, and so on. But 'the state may not use its coercive apparatus for the purpose of getting some citizens to aid others' (*ibid.*: ix). And again: 'taxation of earnings from labour is on a par with forced labor' (*ibid.*: 169). A footnote at this point indicates that Nozick is unsure how 'on a par with' is to be understood. So he should be.

There are several problems with these arguments against taxation beyond a certain minimal level, whether they are made in terms of individual rights or in terms of freedom. First, it is far from clear what is to count as the fruits of an individual's labour, especially in a society with a complex and highly developed division of labour. We have already noted the difficulty of assuming that fruits of individuals' labour are represented by their income before tax. No doubt any individual tax-payer would be better off paying less in tax, other things being equal. But other things would not be equal if the general level of taxation were to be substantially reduced. There would certainly be changes in the costs of goods and services, especially, but not only, those now provided free or at a subsidy, and there is no reason to suppose that all incomes would remain at roughly their present levels. It is naive to suppose that a much reduced level of taxation would necessarily increase the freedom of action of tax-payers in general. Finally, it is far from clear why we should treat the 'freedom', of Hayek's and the Friedmans' arguments, or the 'rights' of Nozick's, as the sole or overriding purpose of government. We will return to this question.

As for the issue of choice, there are several problems with the liberal idealization of choice. First, shortage of financial resources can severely limit the range of choices that are practically available through the market. It is far from clear that the medical services available to most of us on the open market would be superior to those presently provided by the NHS. Secondly, the alternatives are often misrepresented. Continuing with the example of medical services, the alternative to state provision is not so much individual choice as a system based on private insurance. In that case, what is available to most individuals will be determined by the policies of large insurance companies. Once again, it is far from clear that an insurance-based system of financing health service provision would significantly improve the level of choice available to most people in this country. Finally, the contrast between choice and state provision assumes that the absence of choice, and therefore of consumer control, is characteristic of public provision. Public services are indeed often inflexible and unresponsive to the needs of their recipients, but we need not suppose that that is an inevitable feature of public provision. In the last few years, for example, several Labour-controlled local authorities have introduced decentralized systems of housing and social-service administration which are significantly more responsive to consumer demand. The style of liberal argument here is one we encountered above in our discussion of Friedman's and Hayek's case for the market. What is at issue is not a realistic account of markets as they currently exist or of what could reasonably be expected to develop if state services were to be withdrawn. Instead, we are offered a utopian account of 'the market' and its workings. Measured against that utopia, it is not surprising that state provision can hardly compete.

The second line of argument against government provision is that government, even democratic government, is not actually representative of people's interests or desires. Harris and Seldon cite survey evidence to establish this point (Harris and Seldon 1979), but there is also a general argument about the character of government as an institution which we return to in a moment. Since the early 1960s the Institute of Economic Affairs has sponsored surveys to discover whether people would prefer to pay less in tax and more in direct charges in return for education and health services of their choice. What these surveys appear to show is a growing majority in favour of allowing individuals to contract out of state services in favour of market provision, falling support for universal provision of 'free' (i.e. tax-financed) services in health and education, support for a voucher system towards the costs of schooling and private health insurance, and so on. In effect, it seems that there has been growing support in Britain for 'choice' and market provision which (at least before 1979) has not been reflected in the policies of 'representative' government. In fact, as with all survey studies of complex and contentious issues, these findings have to be treated with caution. In a careful re-examination of the figures Judge, Smith, and Taylor-Gooby (1983; cf. Taylor-Gooby 1985, Ch. 2) show that they reflect a far more ambiguous pattern of public opinion than the account by Harris and Seldon suggests.

But liberals also have a more general account of the unrepresentative character of government to fall back on. The argument is partly that political parties represent the views of their activist minorities rather than those of their supporters or the public at large. But this is an instance of the more general claim that government, like the market, is an arena for self-interested activity. Government intervention, in the interests of welfare provision, environmental protection, or whatever, always

> 'establishes positions of power. How that power will be used and for what purposes depends far more on the people who are in the best position to get control of that power and what their purposes

are than on the aims and objectives of the initial sponsors of the
intervention.'

(Friedman and Friedman 1980: 232)

The claim here is not that politicians and civil servants are bound to
pursue base or narrowly selfish interests – although Hayek comes
close to that suggestion in the case of socialist societies in 'Why the
Worst Get on Top', Chapter 10 of *The Road to Serfdom*. Hayek's
arguments on this point are extremely weak, as Wootton shows in
the final chapter of *Freedom under Planning*. They assume first, that
any significant degree of economic planning involves the imposition
of cultural uniformity and political dictatorship, and secondly, that
widely shared values involve 'lower moral and intellectual standards'
(Hayek 1944: 103).

The point of the Friedmans' objection is rather different. It is that
politicians and civil servants use their position to pursue their concerns
and objectives rather than those of the electorate. As a sphere of
individual activity government is utterly different from the market in
this respect. In the latter, the voluntary character of exchange
ensures that individuals further their interests only if they also serve
the interests of others. In the case of government, on the other hand,
objectives are pursued through the exercise of power rather than
voluntary exchange. This characteristic of government accounts for
what Friedman calls 'the fallacy of the welfare state' (Friedman and
Friedman 1980: 145). Welfare programmes involve politicians and
bureaucrats spending someone else's money (the tax-payer's) on
themselves or on others. In the second case the concerns of the
recipients are not the primary control:

'Only human kindness, not the much stronger and more depend-
able spur of self-interest, assures that they will spend the money in
the way most beneficial to the recipients. Hence the wastefulness
and ineffectiveness of the spending.'

(*ibid.*: 147)

Here again, the argument depends on the liberal idealization of
the market and its workings, to say nothing of a touching faith in the
reliability of self-interest. The combination of that idealization and a
simplistic account of the workings of government leads directly to

the following conclusion. Government is inevitably irresponsible and unrepresentative: it should be kept under strict control and relied on as little as possible. We return to the idealization of the market below, and simply note for the present that the liberal case here does not rest on any realistic assessment of what the market is likely to provide if state services are withdrawn.

For the rest, liberals are quite correct to question the myth of popular sovereignty – that government activities in the Western democracies reflect the intentions or desires of the electorate. But then no serious student of politics would analyse the workings of government in such terms, and the account of government as a vehicle for politicians and civil servants to pursue their own purposes is equally simple-minded. It is either plainly false – there are numerous cases of politicians and civil servants resigning or risking dismissal (or worse) because of principled disagreement with the policies being pursued – or else true in the trivial sense that what people do is normally what they have decided to do, so that their actions reflect their purposes at the moment of decision. The latter may be correct but it is also uninformative. It does not tell us what policies governments will pursue or how civil servants will conduct themselves. It is not difficult, for example, to envisage welfare services being organized in such a way that evidence of clients' satisfaction is taken into account in decisions over promotion. This shows that there is no necessary conflict between the career interests of welfare professionals and the welfare of their clients. It may well be that public-service bureaucracies are frequently unresponsive to the needs of their clients, and that many require drastic reorganization. But we should not suppose that these problems are an inescapable feature of government provision.

IX

Freedom, equality, and the market

Our discussion of liberalism noted two significant issues and left
them aside for later discussion. One concerned the idealization of
'the market' and its implications for liberal assessments of public
provision and planning. The other concerned the priority given to
freedom or liberty in liberal discussion of social and economic policy.
The two issues are intimately related in liberal thought. The market
is regarded as a realm in which individuals are free to interact and
exchange as they wish, constrained only by general legal regulations
which apply equally to all participants. In contrast, any form of public
planning is seen as an encroachment on freedom. The opposition
between planning and the market in liberal thought is most starkly
presented in Hayek's argument, running throughout *The Road to
Serfdom* and much of his subsequent writing, that there can be no
half-way house between freedom and planning, that the very project
of state control over any area of economic activity leads inexorably
in the direction of a totally planned society. While some of Hayek's
associates have reservations about that particular thesis, it is clear
that liberalism regards with grave suspicion any form of state interference with, or alternative to, the market.

Although these two issues are central to liberal discussion of social
policy, we have noted closely related issues in connection with
several of the other positions discussed in this book. The essentialization of the market is an important part of Marxist analysis, and
again, in rather different ways, in the works of Marshall, Titmuss,
and Goldthorpe. As for the role of freedom in liberal discussion, this
raises the more general issue of the place of principles in social
analysis which we noted in relation to Marshall's and Titmuss's
treatment of social policy and le Grand's discussion of equality. This
final chapter considers first the essentialization of the market, shared

in various ways by liberals, Marxists, and many others, and secondly, the place of principles in political discussion and the analysis of social conditions.

THE ESSENTIALISM OF THE MARKET

Hayek's thesis that there could be no stable half-way house between the market and a totally planned society has been disputed within the liberal camp. For example, Gray argues that there is no necessary progression from the limited forms of planning advocated, say, by Tony Crosland or those adopted by British governments since the war, to the levels of state control attempted by some of the societies of Eastern Europe (Gray 1984a, 1984b). It was widely disputed when *The Road to Serfdom* first appeared. For example, in a broadly enthusiastic letter to Hayek, Keynes reasserts his commitment to moderate planning:

> 'But the planning should take place in a community in which as many people as possible, both leaders and followers, wholly share your own moral position. Moderate planning will be safe if those carrying it out are rightly oriented in their own minds and hearts to the moral issue. . . . what we need is the restoration of right moral thinking.'

> (Keynes [1944] 1980: 387)

Keynes's patrician response fails to address Hayek's arguments that the great danger of planning lies not so much in the intentions of the planners but rather in the moral and political consequences, quite possibly unintended, of the attempt itself. A more serious objection is the point raised in Pigou's review noted earlier (Pigou 1944). Pigou distinguishes two ways of regulating the numbers working in particular occupations. The state may direct particular individuals, or it may pursue its objectives indirectly by, for example, manipulating rates of pay and other conditions. The one restricts the freedom of movement of particular individuals, but the other need not do so. This example exposes the sleight of hand in Hayek's equation of planning and coercion.

The point here can be generalized. In her careful and measured rebuttal of the major arguments of *The Road to Serfdom* Wootton defines planning as 'the conscious and deliberate choice of economic priorities by some public authority' (Wootton 1945: 12). Planning does not involve the attempt to control everything, as Hayek sometimes suggests, nor does it necessarily involve the temptation to expand the planning apparatus if its objectives are not met. Finally, the choice of priorities does not determine the means to be employed in their pursuit. In fact, we have seen that Hayek makes a similar point when he comments on the danger that coercive measures *may* be introduced in pursuit of otherwise legitimate welfare objectives. The implication here is that the state may, and in Hayek's view should, pursue those objectives through non-coercive means. Of course, there are cases where planning restricts the freedom of particular individuals, but it may also operate on the macro-economic conditions in which individuals make their decisions. Hayek's blanket condemnation of planning and public control (other than the enforcement of general regulations in accordance with the rule of law) as if it invariably comes down to the coercion of individuals is tendentious and highly misleading.

In Hayek's case the identification of planning with coercion is merely the obverse of his equation of freedom and the market. It therefore involves an idealization of the market and the identification of freedom as the primary concern in the consideration of social and economic policy. We return to this second point below. For the moment, notice that there is a significant parallel between the liberal counter-position of the market to public control and the treatment of the issue in Marxism, and in much non-Marxist socialist discussion. We have seen that Marx's account of capitalist exploitation assigns a fundamental role to market relations. Marxist and non-Marxist socialists have complained that markets are anarchic, amoral, wasteful, that they leave too much power in private hands and that they generate indefensible inequalities. Given those views of the market it is tempting to see any move towards the development of non-commodity relations as a move towards socialism. In these terms the provision of free medical services or of subsidized housing and transport, and the public ownership of basic industries would appear as elements of socialism. Marxism therefore tends to treat the welfare state as representing an uneasy compromise between a predominantly capitalist society and limited elements of socialism.

In the one case the market is an index of freedom, and in the other it is regarded with suspicion as a sign of capitalist exploitation and of the anarchy of capitalist production. But for Marxists as for liberals, market and plan are treated as if they represented distinct and incompatible principles of social organization. In both cases, then, any combination of market and plan must appear to be inherently unstable: either we move towards increasing public control or else we must return to market provision through privatization and de-regulation. We have noted similar oppositions between the market and social policy or citizenship at other points in this book. Marshall argues that the principle of citizenship inevitably conflicts with the market principles of a capitalist society. Citizenship and the market represent conflicting principles of social organization, with post-war Britain exhibiting an uneasy compromise between them. Or, again, we have seen how Goldthorpe proposes to analyse the British in-flation of the 1970s as resulting from the strength of a mature work-ing class, on the one hand, and the conflict between the principle of citizenship and the unprincipled inequalities of the market, on the other. Finally, Titmuss presents the market and the principles of social welfare as each tending to undermine the other.

These various positions arrive at their assessments of the market in rather different ways, but they nevertheless share an essentialization of the market and the problems that this generates for social analysis. To write of essentialism in this context is to say that the market is analysed in terms of an essence or inner principle which produces necessary effects by the mere fact of its presence. In this case certain consequences are thought to follow merely from the fact that goods and services are provided through market exchanges rather than in some other ways. Precisely what those consequences are supposed to be, of course, will vary from one of these positions to another: they are anarchic and wasteful, they leave too much power in private hands, they generate indefensible inequalities; they are a realm of freedom and efficiency; they foster a spirit of egoism which under-mines the altruism of social policy; under conditions of wage-labour they are the means of capitalist exploitation; and so on. The diversity of markets themselves and of the consequences that are alleged to follow from their existence may be obscured by reference to 'the market' – as if what is at issue is an institutional structure of interactions with roughly similar properties in all significant cases. Such essentialization of 'the market' is a feature shared by Marxist socialism, vehemently anti-socialist liberalism, and many positions in between. It appears, for example, in the treatment of simple distinctions between market and plan, between private and public provision, between production for profit and production for use, between marketed and non-marketed (commodity and non-commodity) provision, and the like, as if clear and well-understood consequences follow from the choice of one or the other.

The problem is not that such distinctions can never be made, but rather that all too often they mask extremely complex and heterogeneous sets of conditions. What is shared by all markets is little more than the fact that something is marketed in them. Otherwise they are highly differentiated, and there is little point in Marxists, liberals, or anyone else trying to analyse the functioning of 'the market' without further specifiction. Markets always operate under specific institutional conditions, which can vary considerably from one case to another. What is meant by institutional conditions in this context are: the market actors (large corporations, government departments, small businesses, producer and retail co-operatives, private individuals, etc.) and the resources available to them; legislative regulation and other forms of administrative and political controls; customary and other informal constraints on acceptable behaviour; linkages with and spillovers into other markets engaging different actors and controls.

The point is that the consequences of market allocation (of toothbrushes, housing, or old-age pensions) cannot be determined independently of what those institutional conditions are. Consider the markets for housing in Britain. Their consequences depend on the size of the public rental sector, the shortage of alternative suppliers of rented accommodation (except in some specialized sectors), the dominant forms of financing private-sector house purchase, the structure of the building industry and alternative outlets for its services, the existence of differentiated stocks of second-hand housing, links between housing finance and other financial markets, international currency exchanges, government monetary controls, and so on. The example is instructive for several reasons. First, in discussion of housing policy the contrasts of market versus administrative provision, private choice versus public allocation, are too simple to be particularly helpful in themselves. How market or administrative provision, or some combination of the two, works cannot be assessed independently of institutional conditions. Unless those conditions and their consequences are taken into account, arguments for or against market provision are of little value.

Secondly, there are several kinds of public interest in the operations of housing markets – in the quality and availability of housing itself, in their effects on employment in the construction industry, in the progressive or regressive character of personal taxation, in the patterns of investment and savings, and so on. Planning involves central regulation of specified parameters according to some set of priorities. It may be concerned, for example, with the quantity of housing starts and completions, the rate of slum clearance, the number of rooms or space available per person, the provision of toilet facilities and their location in relation to kitchens, and so on. As we noted in our discussion of Crosland's account of relations between government and the economy, government intervention operates by means of particular instruments of control and techniques of monitoring performance. These techniques and instruments are always limited in their objectives and their capacities to achieve them, and by the obstacles they have to contend with. For this reason, amongst others, it is difficult to attach any sense to the notion of a totally planned economy (in which all conceivable parameters and conditions are identified and targeted). Again, public provision can take a wide variety of forms: direct provision (NHS hospital services), provision with a fee for use (swimming pools), public finance and regulation of private provision (the British and Australian general practitioner services provide different examples), and numerous other examples. Generalizations about the impact of public provision on the recipients of their services therefore have little to offer.

So where do these considerations leave us? Liberalism, Marxist socialism, and many positions in between, treat market provision and public control as if they represented distinct and incompatible principles of social organization. We have argued that these generalizations about 'the market' (its anarchy, efficiency, or whatever) or about planning don't get us very far. In a different context, Crosland

made a similar point against some of the Labour left in his limited
defence of private profit (the problem is in the uses to which it is put,
not in its existence) and his argument against nationalization (once
the major public utilities have been taken over) as a general policy.
The behaviour of private industry may be regulated by means other
than direct ownership. In effect, Crosland argues that fiscal and other
indirect controls can turn private profit into an instrument of public
policy. The government, he claims, 'can exert any influence it likes
on income distribution, and can also determine within broad limits
the division of total output between consumption, investment, exports
and social expenditure' (Crosland 1956: 27). On this view the consequences of market allocation cannot be derived from any essence
of the market, since they clearly depend on government policy (or
lack of it). Crosland may have had a simplistic and over-optimistic
conception of government capacities, but it is difficult to deny the
force of his general argument that the working of markets are not
independent of government policy, and that government regulation
of the behaviour of the private sector does not necessarily require the
imposition of direct control.

However, in the context of contemporary Britain, it is more important to turn the argument here against the radicalism of the
right. We noted in the Introduction that naive political radicalism
comes in many shapes and sizes, and that its effects are not all of a
kind. The naive radicalism of some sections of the left has had little
direct impact on the policies of central government. Unfortunately,
the same cannot be said of the naive radicalism of the right. Consider
the privatization and deregulation programme of the present government. No doubt some of the more spectacular sales of public assets
involve an element of cynical political calculation regarding, for
example, their short-term effects on government finances and the
scope for tax reductions. But it is difficult to believe that privatization
and deregulation would be pursued across such a wide range of
public services (from British Airways to refuse collection) in the
absence of some general commitment to the virtues of the market.

In Chapter VIII we considered liberal objections to government
regulation of economic activity and the provision of public services.
Some of these are a matter of principle, raising issues of coercion and
the rule of law. Governments should be responsible for national

defence, the maintenance of law and order, and the establishment of a general framework of laws regulating the conduct of private citizens. They may also be concerned with the welfare of their citizens; for example, by providing amenities of various kinds, health and welfare services, and provision for the disabled. What matters here is the absence of coercion. The state may provide health, education, or transport services, but their use should not be made compulsory, and private services should be allowed to compete with them on equal terms. Other objections concern the alleged irresponsibility of government and the untoward social and political consequences of relying on an interventionist state as a means of promoting welfare. Finally, there are objections based on the supposed incapacity of governments to act effectively in many areas: Hayek's 'epistemological' argument against planning, and the more mundane argument that markets are more responsive to consumer demand than public bureaucracies.

In fact, we have seen that their general arguments in favour of the market and against public control are entirely spurious. The argument from coercion and the rule of law turns on a remarkably restricted view of coercion and an interpretation of the rule of law as meaning little more than that the liberty of the individual, as liberals understand it, must take priority over all other concerns and objectives. We return to that view of liberty below. Again, we have seen that there is no necessary 'logic of the situation' built in to the functioning of an interventionist state, and no reason to suppose that it must inevitably lead to dangerous political consequences. For the rest, there may well be cases where market allocation is preferable to the alternatives (imagine state provision of all private clothing in contemporary Britain), but they hardly amount to an argument in favour of the market in all cases. Likewise, there are certainly cases where state services are costly, inefficient, and unresponsive to the needs of their clients, but it is wrong to suppose that these problems are an inescapable effect of public provision. On these points the liberal argument turns on an idealization of the market and its workings and a highly tendentious account of the character of public intervention.

Indeed, the liberal idealization of the market itself undermines any general argument in favour of privatization. We have seen that in Hayek's view the effective workings of the market depend on the presence of and respect for appropriate traditions, the moral behaviour of capitalists and others in the market place, the restriction of corporations to mere intermediaries of the stockholders' interests, and finally on the rule of law. In fact, on Hayek's own account, corporations do not behave as they should and governments do not respect the rule of law. As for the appropriate traditions and morality, it is surely naive to suppose that they will automatically fall into place the moment significant new areas (e.g. school and hospital cleaning, refuse collection) are opened up to private economic activity. In *Wither the Welfare State* Seldon notes that there were growing systems of voluntary, commercial, and charitable provision of education, health, and housing, before the development of state provision in these areas. He goes on to claim that 'if the state had not been misused to provide education, medicine, housing and pensions, they would have evolved in response to changing individual requirements and technical possibilities' (Seldon 1981, 25). And again: 'voluntary welfare would have developed better than the state' (*ibid.*: 24). Perhaps – but what follows if we do accept Seldon's rosy account? The benign admixture of voluntary, commercial, and charitable provision that might have been, does not exist. It would be foolish to imagine that it can be brought to life simply by abolishing the systems of state provision that have developed in its place. Even on its own terms, the liberal argument for the beneficial effects of relying on the market wherever possible is largely a matter of blind faith.

Returning now to the general argument, there is no necessary opposition between market allocation and public control, and there are numerous different ways in which they may combine. What their consequences will be, cannot be determined simply by reference to general concepts of 'the market' or 'plan', but only by reference to the institutional conditions within which they operate. There are times when Hayek seems to recognize this point. For example, in parts of *The Constitution of Liberty* (especially Ch. 4, 'Freedom, Reason, and Tradition') he suggests that the effective workings of the market depend on the presence of appropriate traditions and moral codes. But in spite of that recognition, his anti-planning polemic achieves its superficial appearance of plausibility by essentializing 'the market' (taking an idealized set of institutional conditions as a norm and identifying any departure as a distortion), by grossly exaggerating the objectives of planning and misrepresenting its techniques. In so far as those on the left and elsewhere in the political arena feel that Hayek (or Friedman) require an answer, it should be one that refuses the simplistic terms in which they pose the problems of public policy.

EGALITARIANISM AND POLITICAL ANALYSIS

Many of the positions examined in this book have made considerable use of principles, such as freedom or equality, in their analyses of British society. In *The Strategy of Equality* le Grand uses the existence of discrepancies between social conditions and the principle of equality as a measure of the failure of egalitarian politics in Britain. Or again, an important part of the arguments of Marshall and Titmuss turn on the interpretation of social conditions in terms of the realization of principles, with citizenship or altruism, on the one hand, competing against the influence of the market, on the other. Finally, Hayekian liberalism analyses social conditions in terms of their consequences for the liberty of the individual. Although the principles invoked in these examples and the ways in which they are used are by no means equivalent, they all raise general issues of the place of principles in the assessment of social conditions and in the evaluation of proposals for change. These issues are most clearly raised in connection with the principles of equality and freedom. The following discussion makes no attempt to argue a substantive case in favour of one or other of these principles. Rather, it suggests that there is a disturbing political naivety in the way they are used by some egalitarians on the left and their liberal opponents on the right.

We begin by recalling le Grand's argument that the 'strategy of equality', the use of public expenditure on social-service provision in pursuit of egalitarian objectives, has played an important part in the development of social policy in post-war Britain (le Grand 1982). Nevertheless, he claims, expenditure on the social services has not produced a significantly more equal society. He concludes that the 'strategy of equality' has been a failure and that it should be replaced by a more radical attack on inequality. In fact there are serious problems with le Grand's argument. First, there is the point, noted in Chapter VI above, that egalitarian considerations have not had the importance that le Grand's argument requires in the development of British social services. The 'strategy of equality' certainly had some impact on British politics, but it has never been the dominant element in British political life. For that reason alone we should expect to find significant discrepancies between the requirements of egalitarian principles and the pattern of social policy provision.

But there are other important problems involved in the use of some general principle as a measure of social conditions. It is perhaps tempting to follow le Grand and many others in using the existence of discrepancies between, say, the principle of equality and social conditions as a measure of egalitarian failure. Imagine a society that realizes the principle of equality (in the sense that all relevant decisions and all distributions, of income, wealth, etc., are egalitarian) but is otherwise just like modern Britain. Then the difference between that egalitarian utopia (if a more equal version of modern Britain is your idea of utopia) appears to provide a measure of egalitarian failure. While that approach may have a certain appeal, we shall see that it seriously oversimplifies what is involved in the analysis of social conditions. It can also lead to dangerously misleading political conclusions.

The trouble with that approach is that it requires us to postulate a society governed by a single organizing principle, in this case, the principle of equality. Now, there are influential forms of social theory that attempt to analyse societies in such terms, and some of them have been discussed in this book. To take a different example, the functionalist sociology of Talcott Parsons treats societies as social systems dominated by central values. Or, again, there are well-known Marxist analyses in which modern capitalist societies are thought to be dominated by the needs of capital or the interests of the capitalist ruling class. Of course, there is a difference between the analysis of society in terms of moral or political principles and analysis in terms of class interests or the supposed needs of capital. But what they share is the idea of society as expressing a single essence or organizing principle.

I have argued elsewhere that it makes no sense to analyse societies as governed by one or more organizing principles. Social conditions depend on a variety of diverse processes and conditions, which are not themselves reducible to any single principle or principles of social organization (Hindess 1986; Cutler *et al*. 1977, 1978). If everything is to be understood in terms of the needs of capital, the principle of the market or of citizenship, or even in terms of some conflict between two or three such generalized explanatory principles, then there is little for social analysis to do beyond the gestural reduction of social facts to the alleged principle of their significance.

There is no need to repeat those arguments here, but it is important to pursue a particular consequence of them. We can usefully begin by asking why it is that some particular inequality is thought to be significant. What we find in *The Strategy of Equality* and many other discussions is that certain inequalities are presented as being obviously significant, and others that could easily be established are ignored. In the case of education, say, inequality is usually presented as if it were a matter of class, or race, or gender, or of geographical differences in provision. But it would not be difficult to identify a number of other educational inequalities. For example, Jencks shows that there may be considerable inequalities between individuals that are not explicable in terms of general social categories such as class, race, or gender (Jencks 1972).

Suppose, to take another example, we were to analyse educational provision by 'ability' – as measured by IQ, examination performance, or informal assessments by teaching staff. The results would show a pattern of gross inequalities that, especially at the levels of secondary and post-compulsory education, clearly favoured the more 'able'. That pattern would not be unrelated to inequalities of class, race, and gender, but it would not be reducible to them. Indeed, what is normally understood by equality of educational opportunity is a systematic discrimination in favour of the more 'able', and without interference from the effects of class and other extraneous elements. Fortunately, and as we should expect from the above discussion, the British education system is far from being a meritocracy in this sense (Halsey, Heath, and Ridge 1980). Nevertheless, it does have significant meritocratic elements, with the result that many of those most in need of educational support are least provided with it.

These examples are instructive for several reasons. First, they show that the reduction of aggregate inequalities between the broad social categories of class, race, or gender is not equivalent to the reduction of inequalities between individuals. Secondly, the promotion of equality in some respects (e.g. equality of educational opportunity) may lead to greater inequalities in others. In fact there is a more general point here; namely, that the consequences of promoting greater equality in some respect will always depend on how the relevant changes interact with a variety of other conditions. Finally, the evaluation of educational provision, or other areas of social policy, in terms of equality invariably selects out certain aspects for attention and concern. In other words, what inequalities are identified as a cause for concern will always be a function of considerations that cannot be derived from the notion of equality itself.

THE PRIMACY OF FREEDOM?

We have seen that planning does not necessarily involve restrictions on freedom in Hayek's sense. Nevertheless, it is clear that many forms of planning do involve restrictions on the freedom of action of individuals or corporations. Are such restrictions on freedom necessarily objectionable? The answers of Friedman and Hayek are clear, but they depend on giving their ideal of a free society priority over all other objectives. In Hayek's usage, freedom means simply that an individual is not subject to coercion by the arbitrary will of another or others. Two consequences of this conception are particularly worth noting. First, freedom in this sense is one and indivisible. Since it is defined as the absence of coercion by others, it follows that any restriction imposed by others is an attack on freedom *per se*. This allows direct economic controls to be represented as a threat to liberty in general.

Secondly, we have already seen that this conception of freedom takes no account of the effects of impersonal restrictions. Poverty and unemployment may severely restrict what an individual is able to do, but since they do not involve coercion by other individuals, such restrictions have nothing to do with freedom. We have also seen that Hayek's discussion of liberty and coercion concentrates on relations between the state and its citizens. The problem here is that the state is by no means the only source of coercion in modern societies. Coercive relationships are a widespread feature of the sphere of paid employment. Freedom of contract in employment means that neither party to a contract is required by law to enter into that particular contract. Freedom of the contract does not rule out coercion within the employment relationship that it establishes. In terms of Hayek's conception of freedom, there is no reason to treat the reduction of legal constraints over economic activity as if it were equivalent to an overall reduction of coercion in society.

Why should freedom, in the rather limited sense in which Hayek and Friedman use the term, be given priority over all other objectives? The above comments on equality suggests two respects in which that priority may be questioned. First, we saw that discussion of equality tended to treat particular patterns of inequality as significant and effectively to ignore others. Different inequalities are not necessarily equivalent in the sense of being equally matters of political concern. In other words, it is equality in some particular respects that is at issue rather than equality in general. It follows that whatever respects are identified as matters of political concern must depend on considerations that cannot be derived from the notion of equality as such. Secondly, to analyse social policies or social conditions generally solely in terms of some principle of equality is to ignore the unavoidable complexity of social arrangements. To the extent that egalitarian concerns have played a part in political life, they have always done so in conjunction with a variety of other concerns, interests, and objectives.

By analogy, we might suggest first that what matters is not so much freedom in general but rather freedom in some particular respects, and secondly, that while a concern for freedom may be one consideration amongst others, it could not be the sole concern in political life. If this approach were to be adopted, then specific restrictions need not be interpreted as attacks on freedom *per se*, and there would be no reason to limit our concerns to restrictions involving coercion by others.

There is a robust discussion of freedom in precisely these terms in Barbara Wootton's *Freedom under Planning*, her response to *The Road to Serfdom*:

'The freedoms that matter in ordinary life are definite and concrete; and they change with the changing ways of different ages and civilizations. Freedom today might mean, for instance, freedom to ask for your cards and sweep out of an objectionable job; freedom to say what you think of the government in language of your own choosing; freedom to join, or to refuse to join, the Transport and General Workers' Union; freedom to start a rival Union on your own; . . . . No one would suggest that all these freedoms are of equal importance; nor do these examples necessarily cover all the freedoms that we actually have, can have, or ought to have.'

(Wootton 1945: 9)

The freedoms listed by Wootton are distinct, but they share a common quality, 'the quality, in fact, of freedom, [the] ability to do what you want' (*ibid.*: 9–10). This approach differs from that of Hayek in two important respects. First, Wootton's concern for freedom is not restricted merely to the absence of coercion. The ability to do some particular thing that you want to do may be restricted by the arbitrary will of others, but it may also be subject to impersonal restrictions of various kinds. Hayek lights on the 'common quality' of Wootton's various freedoms to describe her account as Promethean – freedom as omnipotence: 'Once this identification of freedom with power is admitted, there is no limit to the sophisms by which the attractions of the word "liberty" can be used to support measures which destroy individual liberty' (Hayek 1960: 16). Sophistry indeed! It is a curious argument that seeks to discredit a concept by reference to the sophisms in which it has been employed. We could, for example, respond to Hayek's slur by invoking all those cases where definite freedoms of the kind in Wootton's list have been withdrawn in the name of individual liberty. We could note, for example, that the freedom to join a trades union was withdrawn from civil servants at GCHQ in Cheltenham by a British government committed to extending the liberty of the individual. Such arguments are easy enough to construct, but they establish nothing of any value. For the rest, since Wootton is careful to distinguish between different freedoms, and to suggest that they are not all of equal importance, it is clear that Hayek's response seriously misrepresents her position.

Secondly, Wootton's freedom is not one and indivisible. A restriction on some specific freedom is just that; it is not an attack on liberty as such. Later in her Introduction, she goes on to distinguish broad categories of civil, cultural, political, and economic freedoms. There is no reason in general to suppose that restrictions on freedoms within one of these categories necessarily threaten all the rest. Some forms of economic planning by government may involve restrictions on the freedom of action of individuals or corporations, but there is no reason to interpret that as a threat to liberty in general. Since freedom is not one and indivisible, and different freedoms are not of equal importance, there is no reason to give freedom priority over all other objectives: 'Freedom for everybody to do what he wants is not necessarily the sole purpose of organised society. There may be other admirable ends which conflict with, or demand limitations upon, freedom' (Wootton 1945: 10–11). Since freedoms are not equally important, some limitations may not matter very much. Driving restrictions are a clear example. In other cases, important freedoms may be at stake. Any form of economic planning that involved, for example, widespread direction of labour would be unacceptable in this country. Much of Wootton's book is devoted to considering 'how significant contemporary freedoms are likely to be affected by authoritative public choice of economic priorities' (*ibid*.: 19). There are important issues here that are thoroughly obscured by the insistence that freedom is one and indivisible.

To insist that the ideal of a free society, in the sense of Friedman or Hayek, has priority over all other objectives is to deny that what matters are freedoms that differ in kind and vary in importance. But why should we regard freedom as one and indivisible, such that each and every encroachment must be resisted? What seems to be at stake here is a notion of the inviolability of the person. What unites the different freedoms, then, is the view that restriction of any one of them is a violation of the person and is to be resisted for that reason.

At one point in his *Anarchy, State and Utopia*, Nozick complains that 'there is no shortage of unsupported statements of a presumption in favour of equality' (Nozick 1974: 233). In fact, the same could be said about the primacy of freedom, conceived as one and indivisible, in much contemporary liberalism. Nozick does at least raise the question: 'But why may one not violate persons for the greater social good?' (*ibid*.: 32). His answer contains two elements. One is the claim that, strictly speaking, there is no social good:

'There is no *social entity* with a good that undergoes some sacrifice for its own good. There are only individual people, different individual people, with their own individual lives. Using one of these people for the benefit of others, uses him and benefits the others. Nothing more. What happens is that something is done to him for the sake of others. Talk of an overall social good covers this up.'

(*ibid.*: 32–3)

Methodological individualism, the presumption that the whole of social life is in principle reducible to the actions of individuals, is an eminently respectable position in modern social thought – unfortunately, in my view (Hindess 1977, 1986). But, as Weber insists in *Economy and Society*: 'It is a tremendous misunderstanding to think that an "individualistic" method should involve what is in any conceivable sense an individualistic system of values' (Weber 1968: 18). Even if, in some ultimate sense, there are only individuals, the individuals concerned in particular social entities (Britain, the Labour Party, the working class, or the unemployed) will be a constantly changing population, and reduction to the relevant individuals is unlikely to be a practical possibility in most cases. Commitments to the interests of social entities are not equivalent to commitments to particular individuals. Social goals can survive the appeal to methodological individualism.

The second element is that to

'use a person in this way does not sufficiently respect and take account of the fact that he is a separate person, that his is the only life he has. *He* does not get some counterbalancing good from his sacrifice, and no-one is entitled to force this upon him – least of all a state or government that claims his allegiance and that therefore scrupulously must be neutral between its citizens.'

(Nozick 1974: 33)

This last point is an obvious non-sequitur. For the rest, the reason we may not violate persons for the greater social good comes down to the assertion that we are not entitled to do so. The priority of freedom over all other concerns and objectives is established by mere repetition.

PRINCIPLES AND POLITICAL ANALYSIS

To conclude, we consider the evaluation of governments and policies in terms of equality, freedom, or some other principle. We have argued that governments act by means of specific policy instruments and subject to the limitations of those instruments. Policy instruments can certainly be changed, but at any given time there are limits to the changes that can be introduced and to the costs that can be incurred in bringing them about. Governments are also constrained by the need to maintain at least some level of consent, not only within the electorate but also within state institutions themselves and various outside groups. The inauguration of the NHS, for example, involved important compromises between the government and organizations representing GPs and other medical professionals. The appeal to principles often plays a part in the processes in which decisions are made, followed through, or set aside. But principles are not the only considerations. To make these points is to say that governments act through and by means of existing institutional conditions, and these, together with various outside forces, restrict their room for manoeuvre. Some of those conditions may well be changeable, but at any given time, most of them have to be regarded as more or less fixed.

If society cannot be conceived as organized around a single general principle or set of principles, then governments can hardly be blamed for failing to bring about that state of affairs. Weale suggests that the principle of equality 'may be too demanding a test for any set of institutional arrangements' (Weale 1985: 321). The point applies to any other principle. In fact, a similar conclusion follows even if we do attempt to analyse societies in terms of some principle of social organization. Talcott Parsons, who presents the most sustained and systematic attempt to analyse societies in terms of central values, argues that complete conformity to those values is impossible – the important point here being that societies are invariably subject to exigencies other than those imposed by their central value systems. Similarly, Marxist analyses in terms of the needs or interests of capital, generally invoke contradictory elements – the struggles of the working class, contradictions within capital itself, and so on. Thus, whether societies are seen as organized around central values, the needs of capital, or whatever, deviations from their supposed organizing principles are always to be expected.

Returning now to the principle of equality, we must conclude that inequalities are to be expected and that they will come about for a variety of different reasons. Inequalities on a similar scale are not necessarily equivalent, in the sense of being equally matters of political concern or equally amenable to political action. Except in terms of an ultra-left politics, in which any departure from principle is to be condemned, the fact of inequality has no clear political significance in and of itself. Otherwise, a particular pattern of inequality acquires significance only in relation to some principle of equality and a variety of other considerations. We have argued that similar points apply in the case of freedom. What matters are various particular freedoms and particular constraints upon them. These freedoms are not of equal importance, and actual or potential constraints upon them cannot be evaluated in terms of freedom alone, without reference to a variety of other considerations.

In particular, then, there is no necessary cause for concern in the alleged trade-off between freedom and equality, as if any worthwhile gain on the one side required a corresponding loss on the other. There is no reason to suppose that reduction of significant inequalities necessarily involves the loss of important freedoms, or that the preservation of important freedoms requires inequalities that would otherwise prove unacceptable. The argument here is not that all conflicts between principles can be avoided, or that there are no hard cases in which one principle has to be weighed against another. On the contrary, there will always be disputes between individuals or groups claiming to represent different principles, and cases in which individuals are pulled in contrary directions by the principles to which they try to adhere. The point rather is that the problems of choice that do arise in political life can rarely be reduced to a simple conflict between one principle and another.

There is nothing novel about these points. They are worth raising because of the naive radicalism that we have noted in le Grand's dismissal of the 'strategy of equality', and in some of the conclusions of Goldthorpe, Halsey and Townsend – and also of liberal polemics against even the mildest 'strategy of equality'. What le Grand presents as the 'strategy of equality' is the attempt to use the institutional conditions of British politics to further egalitarian objectives, especially in relation to differences between classes and geographical areas. He dismisses that 'strategy' as ineffective and argues instead for a more radical approach which attacks inequality at its source.

It is not the radicalism of such conclusions that is disturbing, but their political naivety. The most important problem here concerns the failure to address the problems of working for objectives under current political conditions. The importance of emphasizing that a variety of conditions and processes contribute to the maintenance (or otherwise) of particular social arrangements is that it removes the temptation of attributing the non-realization of equality to a single basic cause. That is a temptation to which le Grand appears to succumb in his identification of the 'basic structure of social and economic inequality' (le Grand 1982: 51) ultimately with the ideology of inequality which 'lies behind them' (*ibid.*: 139). Egalitarian politics have not been conspicuously successful in post-war Britain, but it does not follow that a radical alternative to the strategy of equality would therefore be more successful, especially as it remains unclear what that alternative would be.

The political programmes of governments and parties always bring together a variety of distinct concerns and objectives. That means that any one concern, say, with equality, has to compete with others. Priorities may shift between these concerns in response to external conditions and to changes in the balance of forces within the government or party. Egalitarian politics, or any other attempt at significant social change, has to be concerned with winning political support. A radical egalitarian politics that could not influence the programme of an actual or potential party of government and help it win or sustain significant electoral support would hardly be worth considering. There is no practicable alternative to extending the strategy of equality and working to make it more effective. To reject that is not to opt for something more radical. It is to opt for a strategy of abstention.

The attempt to draw conclusions for political action from a study of the distributional impact of public expenditure on the provision of goods and services (or of poverty, social mobility, or educational inequalities) in the absence of serious investigation of the conditions of political action reflects a naivety (or an anti-democratic élitism) that is unfortunately all too common on the left in British politics. Alternatively, and perhaps more charitably, it might be said to result from sociological reductionism in which the institutions, organizations, and ideologies of contemporary politics are seen as reflecting some underlying social reality. Such reductionisms have an important place in many Marxist analyses of political conditions and also, as we saw in Chapter IV, in Goldthorpe's decidedly non-Marxist analysis of the British inflation of the 1970s.

In an earlier discussion of the politics of democratization in contemporary Britain (Hindess 1983), I argued that the assessment of particular conditions (the internal structure of the Labour Party, the management of public-housing estates, or whatever) and of proposals for reform must always be a complex matter in which the question of 'democracy' appears as one element in conjunction with a variety of other considerations. Particular social conditions and proposals for democratization cannot be considered in terms of democracy alone. They should also be considered in relation to a more general politics involving a strategic assessment of current conditions and proposals in relation to some definite set of substantive concerns and objectives. Precisely similar points could be made in relation to equality. It is only in terms of a more complex and general politics that it makes sense to give priority to some inequalities or sources of inequality rather than to others. Likewise, the effectiveness of politics can only be seriously assessed in relation to the conditions in which it operates, on the one hand, and the range of interests and objectives it attempts to pursue, on the other.

To make these points is not necessarily to defend the specific politics of Crosland, Tawney, or others whom le Grand identifies with the 'strategy of equality'. But it is certainly to maintain that we should be wary of rejecting that general strategy of reform that Goldthorpe, in a passage cited earlier, describes as:

'the strategy of seeking to attack social inequalities via legislative and administrative measures of a piecemeal kind that can be carried through without venturing too far beyond the limits of "consensus" politics.'

(Goldthorpe 1980: 252; quoted in le Grand 1982: 125)

No doubt the products of that 'strategy' leave a great deal to be desired. But to make that point is to say that we should work to make it more successful. It is not to say that the strategy should therefore be dismissed, still less that the gestural alternatives are likely to be more effective.

References

Alt, J. (1979) *The Politics of Economic Decline*. Cambridge: Cambridge University Press.

Althusser, L. (1971) Ideology and the Ideological State Apparatuses. In *Lenin and Philosophy and Other Essays*. London: New Left Books.

Arblaster, A. (1977) Anthony Crosland: Labour's Last Revisionist. *Political Quarterly*.

Bacon, R. and Eltis, W. (1976) *Britain's Economic Problem: Too Few Producers*. London: Macmillan.

Barry, N. (1979) *Hayek's Social and Economic Philosophy*. London: Macmillan.

—— (1984) Is There a Road to Serfdom? *Government and Opposition* 19.

Barry, N. *et al.* (1984) *Hayek's 'Serfdom' Revisited*. London: Institute of Economic Affairs.

Beer, S. (1982) *Britain Against Itself: The Political Contradictions of Collectivism*. London: Faber & Faber.

Bevan, A. (1945) Memorandum by the Minister of Health: The Hospital Service, 16 October.

Bosanquet, N. (1983) *After the New Right*. London: Heinemann.

Brittan, S. (1977), The Futility of British Incomes Policy. *Challenge*, May/June.

Buchanan, J. *et al.* (1978) *The Economics of Politics*. London: Institute of Economic Affairs.

Burton, J. (1984) The Instability of the Middle Way. In Barry *et al.* (1984).

Cairncross, A. (1985) *Years of Recovery: British Economic Policy, 1945–51*. London: Methuen.

Cripps, F., Griffith, J., Morrell, F., Reid, J., Townsend, P., and Weir, S. (1981) *Manifesto*. London: Pan.

Crosland, C. A. R. (1956) *The Future of Socialism*. London: Cape.

—— (1967) *The Conservative Enemy*. London: Cape.

—— (1974) *Socialism Now*. London: Cape.

Crossman, R. H. S. (ed.) (1952) *New Fabian Essays*. London: Dent.

Cutler, A. J., Hindess, B., Hirst, P. Q., and Hussain, A. (1977, 1978) *Marx's Capital and Capitalism Today* (2 vols). London: Routledge & Kegan Paul.

Dahl, R. (1985) *A Preface to Economic Democracy*. Oxford: Polity.

Davies, G. and Piachaud, D. (1983) Social Policy and the Economy. In Glennerster (1983).

Demaine, J. (1981) *Contemporary Theories in the Sociology of Education*. London: Macmillan.

Donnison, D. (1979) Social Policy since Titmuss. *Journal of Social Policy* 8.

—— (1982) *The Politics of Poverty*. Oxford: Martin Robertson.

Dworkin, R. (1977) *Taking Rights Seriously*. London: Duckworth.

—— (1981) What Is Equality? *Philosophy and Public Affairs* 10.

Field, F. (1981) *Inequality in Britain: Freedom, Welfare and the State*. London: Fontana.

Fine, B., Harris, L., Mayo, M., Weir, A., and Wilson, E. (1984) *Class Politics: an answer to its critics*, London, Leftover Pamphlets.

Flora, P. and Heidenheimer, A. J. (eds) (1981) *The Development of Welfare States in Europe and America*. New Brunswick: Transaction Books.

Foster, P. (1983) *Access to Welfare*. London: Macmillan.

Friedman, M. and Friedman, R. (1980) *Free to Choose*. Harmondsworth: Penguin.

George, V. and Wilding, P. (1976) *Ideology and Social Welfare*. London: Routledge & Kegan Paul.

—— and —— (1984) *The Impact of Social Policy*. London: Routledge & Kegan Paul.

Glennerster, H. (ed.), (1983) *The Future of the Welfare State*. London: Heinemann.

—— (1985) *Paying for Welfare*. Oxford: Blackwell.

Glyn, A. and Sutcliffe, R. (1972) *British Capitalism: Workers and the Profits Squeeze*. Harmondsworth: Penguin.

Goldthorpe, J. H. (1962) Social Stratification in Industrial Society. In P. Halmos (ed.) *The Development of Industrial Societies*, Sociological Review Monograph 8.

—— (1978) The Current Inflation: Towards a Sociological Account. In Hirsch and Goldthorpe (1978).

—— (1980) *Social Mobility and Class Structure in Modern Britain*. Oxford: Clarendon Press.

—— (1984) The End of Convergence: Corporatist and Pluralist Tendencies in Modern Western Societies. In J. H. Goldthorpe (ed.), *Order and Conflict in Contemporary Capitalism*. Oxford: Clarendon Press.

Gough, I. (1979) *The Political Economy of the Welfare State*. London: Macmillan.

Gray, J. (1984a) *The Road to Serfdom*: Forty Years On. In Barry *et al.* (1984).

—— (1984b) *Hayek on Liberty*. Oxford: Blackwell.

Hadden, T. (1977) *Company Law and Capitalism*. London: Weidenfeld & Nicolson.

Hall, S. (1979) The Great Moving Right Show. *Marxism Today*, January.

Halsey, A. H., Heath, A. F., and Ridge, J. M. (1980) *Origins and Destinations: Family, Class and Education in Modern Britain*. Oxford: Clarendon Press.

Harris, R. and Seldon, A. (1979) *Over-Ruled on Welfare*. London: Institute of Economic Affairs.

Hayek, F. A. (1944) *The Road to Serfdom*. London: Routledge & Kegan Paul.

—— (1960) *The Constitution of Liberty*. London: Routledge & Kegan Paul.

—— (1967) The Corporation in a Democratic Society: In Whose Interest Ought It to and Will It Be Run? In *Studies in Philosophy, Politics and Economics*. London: Routledge & Kegan Paul.

Heclo, H. (1981) Toward a New Welfare State. In Flora and Heidenheimer (1981).

Hendry, D. F., and Ericsson, N. R. (1983) Assertion without Empirical Basis: An Econometric Appraisal of Friedman and Schwarz's 'Monetary trends in . . . the United Kingdom'. In *Monetary Trends in the United Kingdom*, Bank of England Panel of Academic Consultants, paper no. 22.

Hindess, B. (1977) Humanism and Teleology in Sociological Theory. In *Sociological Theories of the Economy*. London: Macmillan.

—— (1981) The Politics of Social Mobility. *Economy and Society* 10.

—— (1983) *Parliamentary Democracy and Socialist Politics*. London: Routledge & Kegan Paul.

—— (1984) Rational Choice Theory and the Analysis of Political Action. *Economy and Society* 13.

—— (1986) Actors and Social Relations. In S. Turner and M. Wardell, (eds) *Sociological Theory in Transition*. London: Allen & Unwin.

Hindess, B. and Hirst, P. Q. (1983) Labour's Crisis. *New Society*, 29 September.

Hirsch, F. (1976) *Social Limits to Growth*. Cambridge, Mass.: Harvard University Press.

Hirsch, F. and Goldthorpe, J. H. (eds) (1978) *The Political Economy of Inflation*. Oxford: Martin Robertson.

Hirst, P. Q. (1979) *On Law and Ideology*. London: Macmillan.

—— (1985) *Marxism and Historical Writing*. London: Routledge & Kegan Paul.

Hobsbawm, E. (1984). Labour's Lost Millions. *Marxism Today*, April.

—— (1985) The Retreat into Extremism. *Marxism Today*, April.

Holland, S. (1975) *The Socialist Challenge*. London: Quartet.

Holloway, J. and Picciotto, S. (1978) *The State and Capital: A Marxist Debate*. London: Edward Arnold.

Hussain, A. (1976) The Economy and the Educational System. *Economy and Society* 5.

Hutton, G. (1956) Review of *The Future of Socialism*. *Spectator*, 12 October.

Jacques, M. and Mulhern, F. (eds) (1980) *The Forward March of Labour Halted*. London: New Left Books.

Jencks, C. (1972) *Inequality: A Reassessment of the Effect of Family and Schooling in America*. New York: Basic Books.

Judge, K., Smith, J., and Taylor-Gooby, P. (1983) Public Opinion and the Privatization of Welfare. *Journal of Social Policy* 12.

Kautsky, K. (1971) *The Class Struggle*. New York: Norton.

Kay, J. A. and King, M. A. (1978) *The British Tax System*. Oxford: Oxford University Press.

Keynes, J. M. (1944) Letter to Hayek, 28 June. In *Collected Writings*. Vol. 27. London: Macmillan, 1980.

Klein, R. (1983) *The Politics of the National Health Service*. London: Longman.

Klein, R. and O'Higgins, M. (eds) (1985) *The Future of Welfare*. Oxford: Blackwell.

Labour Party (1973) *Labour's Programme*. London.

—— (1982) *Labour's Programme*. London.

le Grand, J. (1982) *The Strategy of Equality*. London: Allen & Unwin.

Lenin, V. I. (1964) *The State and Revolution: Collected Works*. Vol. 25. London: Lawrence & Wishart.

Leonard, P. (1979) Restructuring the Welfare State. *Marxism Today*, December.

Lereuz, J. (1976) *Economic Planning and Politics in Britain*. Oxford: Martin Robertson.

Lindblom, C. (1977) *Politics and Markets*. New York: Basic Books.

MacGregor, S. (1981) *The Politics of Poverty*. London: Longman.

Marshall, T. H. (1950) *Citizenship and Social Class*. Cambridge: Cambridge University Press.

—— (1981) *The Right to Welfare and Other Essays*. London: Heinemann.

Marx, K. (1859) *A Contribution to the Critique of Political Economy*. London: Lawrence & Wishart (1971).

—— (1867) *Capital*. Vol. 1. Harmondsworth: Penguin (1976).

Marx, K. and Engels, F. (1848) The Manifesto of the Communist Party. In *Selected Works*. Moscow: Progress (1976).

Matthews, R. C. O. (1968) Why Has Britain Had Full Employment since the War? *Economic Journal* 78.

Meacher, M. (1982) *Socialism with a Human Face*. London: Allen & Unwin.

Miliband, R. (1969) *The State in Capitalist Society*. London: Weidenfeld & Nicolson.

—— (1973) *Parliamentary Socialism*. London: Merlin.

Mishra, R. (1981) *Society and Social Policy: Theoretical Perspectives on Welfare*. London: Macmillan.

—— (1984) *The Welfare State in Crisis*. Brighton: Wheatsheaf.

Morrison, H. (1945) Memorandum by the Lord President of the Council: The Future of the Hospital Services, 12 October.

Nozick, R. (1974) *Anarchy, State and Utopia*. Oxford: Blackwell.

OECD (1981) *The Welfare State in Crisis*. Paris: OECD.

Offe, C. (1984) *Contradictions of the Welfare State*. London: Hutchinson.

Olson, M. (1982) *The Rise and Decline of Nations*. New Haven: Yale University Press.

Orwell, G. (1944) Review of Hayek: *The Road to Serfdom*. In *Collected Essays*. Vol. 3. London: Secker & Warburg, 1968.

Owen, D. (1981) *Face the Future*. London: Cape.

Piachaud, D. (1981) Peter Townsend and the Holy Grail. *New Society*, 10 September.

Pigou, A. G. (1944)) Review of Hayek, *The Road to Serfdom. Economic Journal* 54.

Plant, R. (1984) *Equality, Markets and the State.* Fabian Tract 494.

Poulantzas, N. (1976) *Classes in Contemporary Capitalism.* London: New Left Books.

Pound, R. (1934) Rule of Law. In E. R. A. Seligman (ed.) *Encyclopaedia of the Social Sciences.* New York: Macmillan.

Przeworski, A. (1985) *Capitalism and Social Democracy.* Cambridge: Cambridge University Press.

Rose, R. (1984) *Understanding Big Government: The Programme Approach.* London: Sage.

Scott, J. (1979) *Corporations, Classes and Capitalism.* London: Hutchinson.

Seldon, A. (1981) *Wither the Welfare State.* London: Institute of Economic Affairs.

Sinfield, A. (1978) Analyses in the Social Division of Welfare. *Journal of Social Policy* 7.

Strachey, J. (1956) The New Revisionist. *New Statesman,* 6 October.

Stretton, H. (1983) How the Left Should Think about Home Ownership. *Labour Forum* 5.

Tawney, R. H. (1931) *Equality.* London: Allen & Unwin.

Taylor, R. (1980) *The Fifth Estate.* London: Pan.

Taylor-Gooby, P. (1985) *Public Opinion, Ideology and State Welfare.* London: Routledge & Kegan Paul.

Thurow, L. (1981) *The Zero-Sum Society.* Harmondsworth: Penguin.

Titmuss, R. M. (1958) *Essays on the Welfare State.* London: Allen & Unwin.

—— (1970) *The Gift Relationship.* London: Allen & Unwin.

Tomlinson, J. (1981) The 'Economics of Politics' and Public Expenditure. *Economy and Society* 10.

—— (1982) *The Unequal Struggle? British Socialism and the Capitalist Enterprise.* London: Methuen.

Townsend, P. (1979) *Poverty in the United Kingdom.* Harmondsworth: Penguin.

—— (1981) Reply to Piachaud. *New Society,* 17 September.

Toye, J. F. J. (1976) Economic Theories of Politics and Public Finance. *British Journal of Political Science* 6.

Weale, A. (1985) The Welfare State and Two Conflicting Ideals of Equality. *Government and Opposition* 20.

Weber, M. (1968) *Economy and Society.* Ed. G. Roth and C. Wittick. New York: Bedminster Press.

Wilensky, H. (1975) *The Welfare State and Equality.* Berkeley: University of California Press.

Williams, S. (1981) *Politics Is for People.* Harmondsworth: Penguin.

Wilson, E. (1977) *Women and the Welfare State.* London: Tavistock.

Wootton, B. (1945) *Freedom under Planning.* London: Allen & Unwin.

Wright, E. O. (1980) Varieties of Marxist Conception of Class Structure. *Politics and Society* 9.

Name index

Subject index

45; social division 45–8; *see
also* welfare state
welfare state: alternatives to 1,
4; coercive aspect 1–2;
consensus view of 4–6, 49;
crisis of 1–3; definition of 8,
135; egalitarian principles 2,
45, 85; expansion of 1;
expenditure on 1, 6, 18, 50,
80–5, 90–2, 96–9; failures of
85; future of 2; liberal view of
7, 121, 135; Marxist view of
6–7, 100, 104, 108, 111–16,
148; objections to 4, 5, 121;
redistributive effects 45, 46,
84, 89; restructuring of 116;
social principles 36; *see also*
social services
Welfare State in Crisis, The
(OECD) 1

West Germany 42, 57
Wither the Welfare State
(Seldon) 2, 154
working class: in capitalist
economy 102–03, 110, 115;
and citizenship 50–2;
composition of 104–05;
definition of 104; development
of 53–5; divisions 59;
homogeneity of 53, 54, 56;
maturity of 49, 50, 54–9, 149;
power of 5, 54; unity of 59

*Your Personal Guide to the Future
Labour Offers You* 73

Zero-Sum Society, The
(Thurow) 65